[匈牙利] 本斯·纳内 著　史正永 译

牛津通识读本·

美学

Aesthetics

A Very Short Introduction

译林出版社

图书在版编目（CIP）数据

美学 ／（匈）本斯·纳内（Bence Nanay）著；史正永译.
—南京：译林出版社，2023.8
（牛津通识读本）
书名原文：Aesthetics: A Very Short Introduction
ISBN 978-7-5447-9799-3

Ⅰ.①美…　Ⅱ.①本…　②史…　Ⅲ.①美学　Ⅳ.①B83

中国国家版本馆 CIP 数据核字（2023）第 113955 号

著作权合同登记号　图字：10-2020-535 号

美学　[匈牙利] 本斯·纳内 ／ 著　史正永 ／ 译

责任编辑	陈　锐
特约编辑	茅心雨
装帧设计	景秋萍
校　对	王　敏
责任印制	董　虎

原文出版	Oxford University Press, 2019
出版发行	译林出版社
地　址	南京市湖南路 1 号 A 楼
邮　箱	yilin@yilin.com
网　址	www.yilin.com
市场热线	025-86633278
排　版	南京展望文化发展有限公司
印　刷	江苏扬中印刷有限公司
开　本	890 毫米 ×1260 毫米　1/32
印　张	7.625
插　页	4
版　次	2023 年 8 月第 1 版
印　次	2023 年 8 月第 1 次印刷
书　号	ISBN 978-7-5447-9799-3
定　价	39.00 元

序　言

周　宪

　　"牛津通识读本"系列在国内外读书界均很流行，它几近成为这个时代知识载体的一种象征。系列中的每本书均短小精悍，聚焦某个主题，内容生动有趣，读来令人兴致盎然。译林出版社很有眼光地引进这套丛书，择其适合中国读者阅读的品种加以译介，现已很有规模，令广大读者喜爱。作为一个对美学情有独钟的读者，我一直期待着这套书中的《美学》问世，现在终于读到这一卷，且有机会作序，令人高兴！

　　以我的了解，这套书的作者多为某个知识领域的"大咖"，由他们执笔撰写，权威性和影响力自不待言。但本书作者何方神圣此前我完全不知道，上网搜索后方知本斯·纳内为匈牙利人，博士毕业于美国加州大学伯克利分校，现为比利时安特卫普大学哲学教授，按他自己写的自我介绍，他的专业方向是认知科学和精神哲学，尤其擅长感知研究，美学只是副业而已。不过，副业能做到如此这般，足见他作为欧洲新一代哲学家的潜力。

　　从某种程度上来说，这是一本颠覆性的美学导引著作，至少

1

给人以面目一新的印象。也许正是因为纳内年轻而不受传统美学理念束缚，所以他在本书中提出了一系列颇有创意的美学新观点。这些观点不但反映出国际美学界的思潮动向，同时也体现了美学这门古老的学科在西方正经历着深刻的转型。

　　首先，纳内跳出了传统美学与生俱来的精英主义窠臼，坚持一种鲜明的美学民主立场，并将这一立场贯彻在诸多命题之中。比如，他反对艺术家或哲学家对美学的精英主义理解，强调美学就在我们周遭的日常生活之中，文身或朋克摇滚并不比所谓的高雅艺术低下，许多日常生活的体验其实与审美体验并无本质差异。这一下就打破了美学囿于高雅艺术的限制，转而以一种平等而开放的视角来审视美学。接着，他进一步明确了美学与艺术哲学的不同，因为美学所思考的范围远大于艺术范畴。尽管他所触及的许多研究案例与艺术相关，但他的用心显而易见，那就是美学是对我们现实生活的美学审视、思考和参与。这就与主流的艺术哲学研究大相径庭。往远处说，自鲍姆嘉通开创以来，美学一直以美的艺术为目标，如黑格尔《美学讲演录》中开篇所定义的，美学研究的不是一般的美，而是艺术的美，"这门学科的正当名称却是'艺术哲学'，或者更确切一点，'美的艺术的哲学'"。本书作者的主张明显在颠覆这一德国古典哲学的基本信念。虽然他仍恪守美学这个概念在希腊语中的原初含义，即对感觉经验的研究，但是由此出发，他却与以黑格尔为代表的经典美学分道扬镳。不仅如此，他对美学的理解还与主流的英美分析美学大相径庭，这一主流艺术哲学拘泥于区分艺术与非艺术，将大量精力放在了艺术的定义上，却忘了美学最应该聚焦和参与生活。所以，本书提出了一个有启发性的概念：审美体验即审美参与。

纳内对美学的理解是：美学说到底是一种分析拥有审美体验意味着什么的方法。换言之，美学是一种对审美体验的分析，这正是作者擅长的感知与意象哲学研究领域。他以一种调侃的口气说，一个裁缝对自己手工活儿的体验与立体主义大师莱热的体验别无二致，都可称作审美体验。所以，他主张以一种更具开放性和包容性的美学思考方法来理解美学的社会生活参与性，而不是将美学丢在博物馆、音乐厅等封闭的艺术场合，任其自生自灭。

本书的另一个特色是个性化的写作风格。作者以平易近人的文风和丰富多彩的个人经历，并广泛参照认知科学和心理学领域新的发现，来阐发一些古老的美学原理，或是提出一些新问题。这与许多严肃正经的美学研究所具有的学究气迥然不同，充满异趣，即使是一些难以说明的美学命题，也多半由作者在深入浅出中解决了。这种文风和写法也许正是作者为贯彻美学民主精神所做的一次尝试，不但要在思想观念上体现美学的民主精神，而且要在文风上坚持平易近人，这也是美学真正进入日常生活的有效路径，最终体现出"牛津通识读本"作为一种知识载体之初心。

基于这种美学民主，本书合情合理地提出了一个重要概念——"审美谦逊"。纳内之所以提出这个概念，是想以真正全球性的方式来思考美学。美学民主不但体现在他对精英主义美学观的拒斥中，还呈现在他对非西方美学的敬重中。他写道："我们应该始终意识到我们所占据的文化视角，并谦逊地对待我们的审美评价：把它看作从一个非常具体的文化视角做出的评价。我们很容易在美学上感到骄傲自大，或许正是因为它对我们个人来说太重要了。但这也更是我们应该在审美评价时格外谨慎的原因。如果本书有一点重要启示的话，那就是我们所有人都需要更多的审美谦逊。"这句话在当下读来尤其意味深长——西方中心论或美国中心论仍在流行，不但体现在国际关系上，在学术研究中亦是如此。一个身居欧洲传统之中的美学家怀想全球，以一种"审美谦逊"来看待非西方美学的价值和意义，这不正是文明互鉴精神在美学领域的真实写照吗？

这本书虽没有什么宏大叙事，却在娓娓道来的文字中深蕴了美学的思想力量。我在此不过是谈些先睹为快的读后感而已，这本书的价值还有待更多读者去解读、感悟和发现。

目　录

致　谢

　　非常感谢以下人员对本书早期版本所给的意见评价：尼古拉斯·阿尔泽塔、阿尔玛·巴纳、菲利斯塔斯·贝克尔、康斯坦特·伯纳德、奇娅拉·布罗佐、丹尼斯·比勒、帕特里克·巴特林、丹·卡卫东-泰勒、威尔·戴维斯、瑞恩·多兰、彼得·费泽卡斯、加布里埃尔·费雷蒂、洛兰·吉拉丁-拉韦热、克丽丝·戈芬、劳拉·戈夫、约翰·霍利迪、安娜·一野、拉斯洛·柯塞吉、马格达里尼·库库、罗比·库巴拉、凯文·兰德、杰森·莱丁顿、汉斯·梅斯、马诺洛·马丁内斯、莫汉·马森、克里斯·麦卡罗尔、雷吉娜-尼娜·米翁、托马斯·罗利、萨姆·罗斯、马尔滕·斯廷哈根、雅各布·斯泰斯卡尔、滕璐、杰拉尔多·维埃拉、阿勒特·范·韦斯顿、丹·威廉姆斯、尼克·威尔特舍和尼克·杨，以及一名匿名审阅人。要特别感谢多米尼克·洛佩斯，他读了三个不同版本的手稿。本书的撰写得到了欧洲研究理事会"巩固者"研究基金（基金项目号：726251）、比利时弗兰德研究基金会下属"奥德修斯"基金（基金项目号：G.0020.12N）和科研补助金（基金项目号：G0C7416N）的支持。

第一章

迷失在博物馆

你去博物馆，排半个小时的队，支付了二十美元。然后，你就在那里观看展出的艺术品，但你从中什么也没得到。你努力尝试着，读着艺术品旁边的标签，甚至还购买了音频导游讲解，依然一无所获。你该怎么办呢？

也许你只是不太喜欢这个特定的艺术家。也许你对绘画或者艺术并不是很感兴趣。但在其他场合，你确实喜欢欣赏艺术。甚至喜欢欣赏这位艺术家的作品。甚至可能是同一件作品。但是今天，由于某种原因，这种欣赏没能实现。

听起来很熟悉，对吗？我们都曾为此挣扎过。也许不是在博物馆，而是在音乐厅或睡前看小说的时候。沉浸于艺术中可以获得极大的回报，但也很容易出错。这两者之间的界限区分可能非常细微。

我用这个例子来介绍美学主题，因为我们在这些情况下试图获得的是一种体验，即本书要讨论的一种体验。而且这种无法拥有（却努力想要拥有）的体验，实际上就确定了这种体验是什么,以及它们对我们所有人是多么的重要。

虽然我用了艺术上的例子,但当我们试图从山顶上欣赏风景,或者当我们试图尽情享受一顿美食却徒劳无功时,这种情况也会发生。(针对艺术、自然或食物)的审美参与可能是一场艰难之旅。

非精英美学

美学讨论的是某些特殊类型的体验,并且我们对此非常关心。"aesthesis"这个希腊语单词的意思是知觉;而且当德国哲学家亚历山大·鲍姆嘉通(1714—1762)在1750年引入"美学"这一概念时,他的意思正是对感官体验的研究。

美学所讨论的体验十分多样。我们对某些体验的关注基于其他体验。不仅仅是对博物馆的艺术作品或歌剧表演的体验,还有我们下班回家路上对公园里秋叶的体验,还有对哪怕只是落在餐桌上的落日余晖的体验。但是,当你选择今天要穿的衬衫时,或者当你在想是否应该在汤里放更多的胡椒粉时,你这时的体验也是美学所要讨论的。美学无处不在。它是我们生活中最重要的方面之一。

美学有时被艺术家、音乐家甚至哲学家视为过于精英化。这种观点建立在对该主题的一种误解之上,而本书正是要纠正这一误解。所谓的高雅艺术对美学的要求并不比情景喜剧、文身或朋克摇滚更高。而美学的范围远比艺术的范围更加广泛,不管它是高雅艺术还是低俗艺术。美学包含了我们生活中所关心的很多东西。

波兰先锋派小说家维托尔德·贡布罗维奇(1904—1969)

非常优雅地表达了这种观点：

> 一流餐厅的食物并不总是最好吃的。对我来说，当艺术以一种不完美的、偶然的、支离破碎的方式出现，以某种方式暗示它的存在，让人们通过笨拙的诠释去感受它时，它几乎总是表达得更有力。我更喜欢街上从敞开的窗户里传来的肖邦的音乐，而不是音乐会舞台上演奏得气派十足的肖邦的音乐。

美学的工作并不是告诉你哪些艺术品是好的，哪些是坏的。美学的工作也不是告诉你在街上听肖邦还是在音乐厅听肖邦的体验是值得的。如果一种体验值得你拥有，它就会成为美学的潜在主题。你可以在找到这种体验的地方获得你的美学享受。美学并不是一种野外工作指南，告诉你哪些体验是允许的，哪些是不允许的。这也不是一张能帮你找到它们的地图。美学是一种分析拥有这些体验意味着什么的方法。美学是，而且也应该是完全不带批判性的。

这里有一个发人深省的例子。法国画家费尔南·莱热（1881—1955）曾描述他和他的朋友如何观察一位裁缝店老板在橱窗里摆放十七件背心，并配上相应的袖扣和领带。裁缝在每件马甲上花了十一分钟。他把它向左移了几毫米，然后走到商店前面看了看。接着回去，又向右移动一点，如此不断地调整。他太专注了，甚至没有注意到莱热和他的朋友在看着他。莱热觉得有些惭愧，他在想，很少有画家像这位老裁缝一样，对自己的作品抱有如此浓厚的审美兴趣。那些去博物馆的人对作品所抱有的兴趣肯定就更少了。莱热的观点，也是这本书的指导原则，是裁缝的体验与任何到博物馆参观的人欣赏莱热绘画的体验一样，都值得被称为审美体验。

以这种包容性的方式思考美学，为理解我们审美参与的社会层面，以及审美价值对我们自身的重要性这些老问题开辟了新的途径。它也使我们有可能以一种真正全球性方式来思考艺术和美学，而不是以西方的主导地位为前提。

美学还是艺术哲学？

美学不同于艺术哲学。艺术哲学是关于艺术的。美学则包括艺术在内的许多事物。但是它也关乎我们对令人惊叹的风景或办公室对面墙上阴影图案的体验。

本书是关于美学的。因此，它的内容范围比一本关于艺术哲学的书更加宽泛又更为狭窄。艺术哲学讨论各种各样的哲学问题，涉及艺术的形而上学、语言学、政治、伦理问题。这些问题中的大多数我都不会触及。比如，我不会谈论艺术的定义，不讨论艺术品与世界上所有其他物品有什么不同。

美国抽象派画家巴内特·纽曼（1905—1970）曾说过，美学对于艺术家来说，就像鸟类学对于鸟类一样，都是无关紧要的。应该明确的是，在这种公然挑衅的语言中，与鸟类学等同的是艺术哲学，而不是美学。对艺术品进行分类并仔细思考不同种类/类型之间差异的是艺术哲学，而不是美学。因此，纽曼的这句俏皮话实际上是关于艺术哲学的，而不是美学。美学研究的正是艺术家们工作时的体验以及他们试图唤起的体验，它与每一个艺术家都息息相关。

艺术品自然可以触发各种各样的体验,但美学实际上无法谈论所有这些体验。我相信一个艺术品小偷对其所偷的艺术品有某种体验,但这不太可能是本书所讨论的这种体验。或者设想一下:我承诺给你一大笔钱,让你跑遍整个大都会艺术博物馆数一数有多少幅画签了名。我相信你可以做到,但这并不会让你处于一种审美状态——不管人们理解的这种审美状态多么宽泛。

我们与艺术品进行审美接触,但我们也以其他各种方式与艺术品接触。而且与我们进行审美接触的还有许多其他事物。(在整本书中,我或多或少地将"审美体验"和"审美参与"混为一谈,承认审美参与是我们所做的事情,而审美体验则是我们在审美参与时的感受。)艺术和美学之间的关系是分离的。但这并不意味着我们应该完全忽略这种联系。我们许多有美学价值的时刻都来自对艺术的接触。

换句话说,艺术是一个重要的审美对象,但它绝不是享有特权的审美对象。根据"西方"美学中一个有影响力的分支,我们与艺术的审美接触,也即与高雅艺术的审美接触,和我们与其他事物的审美接触是完全不同的。这种思想不仅因为其限制了审美时刻在我们生活中的重要性和相关性而贬低了美学,而且它违背了几乎所有的非西方美学传统。本书乃一本美学简介,而非对某个非常具体的西方美学传统进行介绍,哪怕它在历史上很重要。

非"西方"美学

世界各地都有工艺品,还有音乐,以及故事。尽管如此,当你进入世界上几乎所有大型艺术博物馆,很可能会遇到产于"西方"的物件（即欧洲的，而且如果是在一座现代艺术博物馆，也许会有北美的——我会在整本书中的"西方"一词上使用引号，以表明"西方"显然不是一个统一的概念）。如果你要寻找来自世界其他地方的物件，经常得要去一个偏远的翼楼，有时甚至要去一个不同的博物馆。但是，无论是艺术还是美学，都不是"西方"的一种专利品。

世界各地的人都在从理论上阐明我们对艺术的体验。坚持欧洲的美学路线就像在博物馆里只展示欧洲艺术品一样带有偏见。伊斯兰、日本、中国、印度尼西亚、非洲、苏美尔–亚述、前哥伦布时代、梵语和巴厘岛的美学都是非常复杂的思想体系，充满了对艺术品和其他事物体验非常重要的观察。任何关于美学的书都不应该忽视它们。

事实上，"西方"美学在很多方面都是不入流的局外人，它强调（或者我应该说是沉迷于？）评判高雅艺术，并将审美参与从社会环境中剥离出来。我不打算自诩在这本书中要涵盖所有的美学传统，但我也不会关注那些明显无法与世界其他地区产生共鸣的"西方"独有的观点——不管提出这些观点的已故白人男性学者的声望如何。

6

第二章

性、药物与摇滚

在某种意义上，能算作审美的体验是多种多样的。不仅仅是听你最喜欢的歌或看你最喜欢的电影，而且还包括在视频网站上观看了一个"最伟大的进球"剪辑，最终决定（购买）一双鞋，选择咖啡机在厨房柜台上的确切位置。要找到所有这一切的共同之处相当困难。

当然，不应该太过包容。哲学家经常将艺术体验与药物诱发的体验和性刺激的体验（以及一般的享乐主义体验，比如狂欢派对，就是摇滚这个术语所描述的这种体验）进行对比。所以，传统的美学思维方式是，我们必须在审美和非审美之间划清界限，因此性和药物就被排除在外，而发型和音乐则包含在内。为何会变成这样呢？

我以性、药物和摇滚问题为背景，介绍美学中最重要的方法。实际上，我认为我们无法断言在审美体验与性、药物和摇滚之间存在区别。所有的事物都能够以一种审美的方式来体验，比如，一些药物引起的体验就可以算作审美（体验）。不过，梳 7

理这些美学方法有助于我们看清楚,将审美和非审美分开是多么困难。

我将讨论美学中四种有影响力的解释,重点谈美、愉悦、情感以及"因其自身原因而具有价值"。不仅仅是为了排除它们或者表明它们不起作用,也不是要取笑它们,我之所以会讨论它们,是因为它们中的每一个都包含了一些非常重要的提示,告诉我们应该怎样以及不应该怎样对美学领域进行探讨。

是美吗?

关于美学,人们最普遍的看法是它关乎美(beauty)。只要在街上环顾一下,就会毫不意外地发现"美学"一词在美容院。而且,当试图解释美学这一哲学学科是关于什么的时候,人们很容易采取类似于美容院的方法。普遍的看法是,有些东西是美的,有些则不然。美学帮助我们把它们区分开,甚至可以解释为什么美的事物是美的。

我称之为"美容院方法",因为在整容手术或美甲行业中,对什么是美什么不是有着相当清晰的概念。事实上,其主要目的是把不那么美的东西变得更美。许多认为美学是关于美的人都有类似的假设,即世界上美的事物和不美的事物之间存在一条分界线。

美容院方法毫不费力地解决了性、药物和摇滚问题。审美体验是对美的事物的体验。药物诱发的体验、性体验,或者摇滚体验,都不是对美的事物的体验。因此,它们不会被视为审美(体验)。

我们很容易嘲笑这种观点的道德性和批判性意味(摇滚是

8

魔鬼的音乐；大麻是魔鬼的收获；而性呢，就是性而已）；但重要的是，美容院方法的真正问题不在于它以一种精英的或者拘束的方式在美与非美之间划清界限。真正的问题是，它任意地画出了这样的分界线。

比如，美和红色是截然不同的。我们可以把世界上所有的东西分成两类：红色的和非红色的。这可能不太合理，但我们能够做到这一点。但是，我们不能把世界上所有的事物分成美的和不美的两类。至少在我们想让美与美学有任何关系时无法做到这一点。就像奥斯卡·王尔德（1854—1900）说的那样，"没有一件东西丑到在一定的光影条件下或与其他东西接近时，还会显得不美；没有一件东西美到在一定条件下看起来还不丑"。

问题在于，美并不是事物的这样一种特征——在任何时候、任何情境下，对所有观察者来说都保持不变。如果这个概念在美学中哪怕略有一点点用处，它就需要能够捕捉到美转瞬即逝的特点以及这样一个事实：就像奥斯卡·王尔德恰到好处地指出的那样，我们有时看到一个物体是美的，有时却看不到。这与"情人眼里出西施"的争论无关——我会在第五章中再讨论这个问题。即使美不是出于观察者的眼中，即使它在某种意义上是"客观的"，它对于我们遇到它的情境也是高度敏感的。美容院方法无法解释这种情境敏感性。

尽管美容院方法在"西方"美学史上占据了主导地位，但就美而言，它并不是唯一的方法。这里有另一种说法，可概括为一个简洁的口号——它错误地（但始终）被认为是孔子（前551—前479）所说："万物皆有动人之处，然非众人皆能洞悉。"因此，我们没有两堆事物，美的和不美的各为一堆。我们只有一堆。

各种先锋派也支持这种观点的不同版本。再回到莱热，他也反对任何形式的"审美等级"。下面是他的一段引人深思的话：

> 美无处不在：也许更多地体现在你厨房白墙上炖锅的摆放上，而不是在你18世纪风格的客厅或官方博物馆里。

因此，任何事物都可以显得美，而美学正是关于这些美的体验。但是，一种体验具有美感，并不是因为我们所体验到的事物是美的，而是因为我们以某种特定的方式来体验它（我们以美的方式体验我们所体验到的任何事物）。重要的不是我们经历了什么，而是我们经历的方式。

这种方法抓住了我一开始提到的反精英主义和非评判性观点，不过这里存在一个花招。这种把美与美学联系起来的方式，实际上让美这一概念变得多余。我们可以不谈美而讲好这个故事。美只不过是我们体验特征的一个占位符——而且也不是一个非常有用的占位符。如果美学是关于事物——无论什么事物——的美的体验，那么我们就会想知道这意味着什么。我怎么做到这一点呢？我在博物馆里看一幅画，但我的体验绝不是审美。我如何将其变成一种审美体验？体验它的美？这不是一个很有帮助的建议。

美容院方法至少给我们提供了一种区分审美体验和非审美体验（比如，依其陈述，对性、药物和摇滚的体验）的方法。这不是一个很好的方法，但仍不失为一个方法。我把美与孔子和莱热相联系的那种更为民主的方式，其本身并不能告诉我们多少关于审美体验的东西。如果我们沿着这条思路走下去，我们仍

10

然需要煞费口舌地解释是什么让某些（而不是其他）体验成为审美体验。如果我们能解释这一点，那么在这方面提及的任何"美"都将只是一个不那么有用的标签。

尽管如此，民主版的美的描述教会了我们一些非常重要的东西。这并不是说有些东西是美的，有些则不是。所有的事物（好吧，几乎所有的事物）都可以触发审美参与。没有任何东西（即使是最伟大的艺术品）能永远做到这一点。最大的问题是我们如何解释这种审美参与以及它的触发方式。你可以用"体验它的美"这个标签作为一个有用的提示，提醒这种体验像什么。但这并非是这种体验的一种解释。

同样的对象，我们可以体验到美，也可能体验到不美。前者是一种审美体验，后者则不是。美描述应该为这种差异提供一种确切的解释。这种解释可能会与这种体验发生的方式有关，或者可能与我们的注意力或情绪的调动方式有关。但这与美并没有多大关系。

是愉悦吗？

另一个常被用来区分审美和非审美的重要概念是愉悦。一般认为审美关乎愉悦，而非审美则不然。审美体验是（经常是——很显然并非总是）令人愉悦的体验，这就是为什么我们喜欢拥有这种体验。我们希望，如果我们能理解体验所包含的愉悦感，就能理解是什么让一种体验具有美感。

并非所有的愉悦都是审美体验。伊曼努尔·康德（1724—1804）详细地论证了审美愉悦的独特之处在于它是无利害的。人们写了数百万页内容，讨论这种"无利害的愉悦"可能的意

11

义。我想从愉悦的心理状态开始，而不是从康德的学术开始。

心理学家将愉悦分为两种。第一种愉悦是当不愉快的事情告一段落时你的感受。我将其称为"解脱的愉悦"，因为它是在身体经过一段时间的扰动后恢复到正常状态时所触发的。所以，如果你饿得很厉害，终于吃了点东西，你感受到的愉悦就是解脱的愉悦——你的身体会恢复到饥饿前的正常状态。

解脱的愉悦是短暂的。我们结束了不愉快的事情——愉悦是解脱时刻的标志。但这只是一瞬间。放松的愉悦并不能激励人。它可能是我们做某事产生的结果，但它不会让我们做进一步的事情。

可以把这种愉悦与我称之为"持续性愉悦"的另一种感受进行对比。持续性愉悦激励我们继续做我们正在做的事情，它维持着我们的活动。我们沿着海滩散步，非常愉悦。这不是一种解脱，只是感觉舒服。与解脱的愉悦不同，它可以持续很长时间，而且它激励我们继续散步。

就像加拿大哲学家莫汉·马森（1948—   ）基于这些心理学区别指出的那样，同一种活动可以在某些情况下给你带来解脱的愉悦，而在另外一些情况下给你带来持续性愉悦。饮食就是一个很好的例子。当你一天没吃东西后吃第一口食物时，它可以给你带来解脱的愉悦。但是，如果你正在享受一顿美食，它也能给你带来持续性愉悦。

审美愉悦是一种典型的持续性愉悦。当你看着一幅画时，你所感受到的愉悦会激励你继续看下去。就像沿着海滩散步一样，这是一项无限制的活动。我们的愉悦维持着我们与这幅画的持续接触。有时候，我们甚至很难逼迫自己离开（这幅画）。

这给我们带来了一个关于性、药物和摇滚问题的复杂情形。一些性和药物诱发的活动会给我们带来持续性愉悦。因此，我们不能完全拒绝性和药物，把它们排除在审美活动的精英圈之外。我认为这是该理论解释的一个优点——我不明白为什么一些性和药物诱发的体验不能算作审美体验。这种愉悦解释甚至给我们一种提示，指出是什么让某些而不是其他由性和药物引发的体验符合条件，也就是说，可算作持续性愉悦。

有相当多的心理学研究讨论了持续性愉悦如何激发和帮助当前进行的活动。喝酒就是一个例子。如果你大量饮用了你喜欢的一种酒水，那么就可以产生持续性愉悦。你在啜饮一口的过程中感到很快乐，也许你会把它含在嘴里打旋，咽下去，再啜一口，依此类推。它有一定的节奏，你在这个活动中获得的愉悦维持了这种节奏，而且还会对这种节奏进行微调。

我们知道很多有关饮酒的生理机制——不同肌肉的同步运动如何造成饮酒过程的无缝协调。但就审美参与而言，这是如何发生的呢？我们颈部肌肉的活动会有什么同等效果？毕竟，没有肌肉直接参与大多数的审美活动。

持续性愉悦通过控制我们的注意力来激发和微调我们正在进行的审美参与。大多数审美活动中都没有肌肉的直接参与，但有大量的注意力参与其中。当你看着这幅画时，你从中获得的快乐会促使你的注意力继续参与其中。因此，将审美愉悦描述为持续性愉悦，应当阐明我们的注意力在审美参与中是如何发挥作用的。

我们应该真正阐明持续性愉悦维持何种注意力的一个重要原因来自女权主义电影理论。英国电影理论家劳拉·穆尔维

（1941— ）在她极具影响力的文章《视觉愉悦和叙事电影》中指出，主流电影几乎总是试图触发"视觉愉悦"，这是典型的男性窥私癖的视觉愉悦。影片鼓励观众认同的主要人物往往是男性，我们也经常受到鼓励去通过男性主角的视角来看待这些电影中的女性。正如马尔维所说，这种高度性别歧视的"男性凝视"构成了叙事电影的视觉愉悦。

无论如何，这种"视觉愉悦"都是持续性愉悦（它鼓励我们继续观看），但它明显不同于美学所说的那种无利害的审美愉悦。因此，愉悦解释需要讲得更多，才能把审美愉悦和非审美愉悦区分开来。不过，这种解释很大程度上与愉悦所维持的心理活动有关，而心理活动又与我们所关注的事物（以及我们的关注方式）有很大关系。

是情感吗？

解释美学领域的第三种方法聚焦于情感。一般认为，审美体验是情感体验。因此，理解审美体验与其他体验的不同之处，就是要理解此处触发了什么样的情感。

爱尔兰小说家艾丽丝·默多克（1919—1999）把文学（和一般艺术）视为一种"激发特定情感、训练有素的技巧"。20世纪最具影响力的一位艺术史学家乔治·库布勒（1912—1996）曾这样说过，讨论艺术的一种简单方式就是把它看作"一种情感体验对象"。作为对艺术的社会学评估，这句话在1959年刚由库布勒写下时听起来可能要比在2019年更有说服力。毕竟，很多当代艺术都尽量远离我们的情感，更倾向于仅仅让智力参与，或者有时仅仅让感知参与（比如概念艺术和光效应艺术）。但是，如果我们把默多克和库布勒的主张看作对审美参与的讨论而不是对艺术的讨论，那么这就相当于把审美体验视为情感体验。

问题是：这涉及什么样的情感呢？所有审美参与中的情感每次都是同一种情感吗？或者根据我们参与的内容以及我们参与的方式不同，而有不同的情感？

更为极端的观点认为，我们在所有审美参与过程中每次都有相同的情感。如果我们有这种情感，那么这就是一种审美参与；如果我们没有情感，那就不是（审美参与）。但是，这种"审美情感"是什么呢？这里不乏各种候选项，从好奇和感动到对形式特征的思考等。不过，我们很容易找到很多任何一种情感都不存在的审美参与案例。

审美参与的一个显著特征就是多样性：我们对科罗拉多大峡谷和比莉·哈乐黛歌曲的审美体验总会包含截然不同的情感。如果我们在所有这些情况下只寻找一种笼统的情感，那就等于忽视或掩盖了美学的多样性。

即使是同一件物品，在不同环境下也会引发颇为不同的情感。关于艺术，我听说过的最奇怪的一个故事来自我的一位要好朋友，她在每一次首次约会后都会去旧金山现代艺术博物馆，坐在一幅非常大的马克·罗斯科绘画前，以想象出她对潜在新恋人的感觉。这可不只是一个用来思考某人的环境，她还要对这幅已受她之前的体验影响过的画做出反应。她告诉我，这幅大型抽象画在这些场合唤起的情感是截然不同的。如果一幅画的审美体验可以导致如此多样的情感，那么如何能够把所有的审美参与都置于一种特殊的"审美情感"统称之下呢？

尽管如此，不可否认的是，审美参与可能是而且也经常是一种情感事件。艺术可以让你哭泣，而且大自然也可以。美学和情感之间的联系是所有美学传统所讨论的东西，从伊斯兰和梵语到日本和中国美学都是如此。

任何对审美体验的描述都需要严肃对待情感，但这并不意味着情感是审美体验成败攸关的条件。只有审美参与是有情感的吗？显然不是。性、药物和摇滚可能让人情绪非常激动，甚至可能比我使用的一些审美体验的例子更富有情感。而且可以这么认为，我们做的每件事在某种意义上都注入了情感。因此，在寻找审美的特殊之处时，强调情感不会有太大帮助。

相反地，审美参与总是富有情感的吗？葡萄牙诗人和作家费尔南多·佩索阿（1888—1935）将自己的审美体验描述为"游离于思想和情感之外，只关注我的感官"，这听起来像是一种熟悉的审美参与形式——情感居于次要地位。至少在某些审美体验的案例中，占主导地位的是感官，而不是情感。

甚至对形式特征的思考，即所谓"审美情感"的一个例子，也可能被认为是一种感知，而无关情感。例如，美国艺术评论家苏珊·桑塔格（1933—2004）将审美体验描述为"超然的、宁静的、沉思的、情感自由的、超越愤慨与赞同的"。

情感或许并不能使审美体验具有美感。但是，美学的情感描述仍然很重要，因为它们强调了情感如何成为审美体验的决定性部分。任何关于美学的描述都需要讲述一个关于情感体验和审美体验是如何交织在一起的故事。

是其自身原因吗？

苏珊·桑塔格认为审美体验是超然的。不仅脱离情感，也

16

要脱离愤慨、赞同和实际考量。这是最后一个区分审美和非审美且很受欢迎的候选项：审美参与就是为了参与而参与。我们这样做不是为了达到一些其他的更进一步的目标。我们这样做只是为了审美刺激。

这个提议有许多特点。有些人讨论了为事物自身原因而具有价值：当我们有一种审美体验时，我们是出于其自身原因而重视我们所体验的事物（或者可能是审美体验本身）。我不会对这种推理过程做太多评价，因为我甚至都不确定我们在审美体验时是否重视某种东西，更不用说出于事物本身原因而重视它了。无论如何，这都取决于一个人对价值的描述，因此我绝对不会打开这里放置的那一罐蠕虫。当我凝视着一束阳光中飞舞的尘埃时，我看重的是什么？那些尘埃？还是我自己的体验？"重视自己的体验"到底意味着什么？意味着我想要拥有它？为它竖起大拇指？如果我们能够在不依赖于价值概念的情况下形成"为其自身原因"的描述，我们确实应该这样做。

不过，我们可以避开价值不谈，只专注讨论我们在审美参与时为什么要做我们正在做的事情。我们是为了达到别的目的，还是仅仅为其自身原因（审美参与）而这样做（参与）？如果我读小说是为了能通过文学课上的考试，那么我做这件事（读小说）是为了达到其他目的（通过考试）。如果只是为了阅读而阅读，那就更接近美学领域。不过，即使我是因为上文学课而开始读这本书的，也会有审美体验。在这种情况下，我做这件事并不是纯粹为其自身原因，尽管如此，我仍然会与它进行审美接触。这并不意味着我的参与就一定缺乏美感。这些中间案例表明，"为其自身原因而做某事"并不是美学的圣杯。

这是表达"为其自身原因"直觉的另一种方法。有些活动只有在到达终点或达成目标时才有意义。完成它们是为了达到某种目的。它们应该被完成。你不能只完成一小部分。比如，在四小时内跑完马拉松。

对于这类活动，有两个选择。你要么实现目标，要么没有实现目标。如果你没有实现，那么你受挫的欲望会产生更强烈的欲望——而这很可能也会受挫。如果你实现了目标，那么四小时跑完马拉松就成了失败者，跑进三小时四十五分钟成了新目标。然后是三个半小时，如此等等。总会有一座更高的山要去攀登。

幸运的是，不是所有的活动都是这样。另有一些可以只完成一小部分的活动。即使没有完成它们，也有意义。这样做并不是为了实现目标。比如，为了跑步而跑步。

有些事你是为了奖品而做的；有些事则是为了过程本身。两者我们都需要。极少有人能在工作中享受所做的一切，且没有任何压力去实现任何目标。总会有要实现的目标、截止日期和晋升标准。

而且，甚至在我们的业余时间里，我们做的很多事情都是为了某种非常具体的目标。我们烹饪一顿饭的最终目的是招待我们的朋友，而不是漫无目的地烹饪。因此，我们无法回避那些为了取得成就而进行的活动。但是，我们需要在为取得成就而进行的活动和为过程本身而进行的活动之间保持一种合理的平衡。

审美参与不是一种奖励型活动。如果进展顺利，它就是一种过程型活动。你这样做不是为了获奖。即使没有达到目标或

18

终点——因为它就没有（设立）目标或终点，这样做也是有意义的。你可以仅仅蜻蜓点水般地看一幅画。这种活动没有自然（或非自然）的终点。审美参与是一种开放式的活动。

任何关于审美参与的描述都需要解释这一重要特征：它是开放式的，且是一个过程，而不是一种奖励型活动。但这也不会成为区分审美与非审美的界限标志。我一直在关注像看一幅画这样确实没有活动终点的案例。但在其他审美参与的例子中，则有一个终点。奏鸣曲和电影都有一个非常自然的终点，也就是在它们结束的时候。我们可以在它们结束后再去思考它们，但从某种非常重要的意义上来说，体验本身是有终点的。在这方面，这些审美活动与永恒的绘画沉思大不相同。

因此，虽然过程型活动是某些审美参与案例的一个重要特征，但它并不是所有审美参与的普遍特征。我们可以在审美参与的范畴内做出区分，有些具有目标导向，有些则无。但缺乏目标导向性并不是这一类别的定义特征。

性、药物和摇滚问题对我们来说意味着什么呢？就像以快 19 乐为中心的说法一样，强调为做事情而做事情的观点也把性和药物诱发的体验分成了两个类别。阿道司·赫胥黎（1894—1963）写了一整本书，讲述了他如何摆脱自己的药物诱发体验，其方式与审美体验的摆脱方式完全相同。再一次强调，我认为这是看待性和药物问题的正确方法，其中一些应该是美学领域的一部分。尽管如此，美学的四种标准方法仍然没有给我们明确地描述这个领域的起点和终点到底在哪里。

这种"为其自身原因"的说法清楚地抓住了审美体验的一个重要特征，但这不是唯一的重要特征。无论审美和非审美之间的最终区别是什么,它都需要抓住以一种开放无限制的方式、为做事本身而去做事情的重要性。

是注意力吗?

我们从美的描述中可以学到的是,如果我们把美容院方法放在一边,那么美学通常就是讨论体验事物之美,而美则是我们体验的某些特征的占位符——需要某种美学描述来填补。以情感为中心的描述强调了情感在我们体验中的重要性,但它仍然需要弄清楚审美体验是如何受到情感影响的。

以愉悦为基础的描述强调了持续性愉悦的重要性,但是如果它们没有具体说明这种持续性愉悦涉及什么形式的注意力,那么它们就是不完整的。而"为其自身原因"的描述,只要我们抛弃价值概念,就会再三强调开放无限制的、超然独立的过程型活动的重要性。

我认为这些描述都指向了同一个方向,即美学的特殊之处在于我们在审美体验中运用注意力的方式。这可以帮助我们解释体验事物之美是如何获得审美资格的,以及是什么让这些体验充满情感。以愉悦为基础的描述缺少了注意力内容,而对注意力超然独立、开放无限制运用的讨论,表达了"为其自身原因"描述的主要内容。正如马塞尔·普鲁斯特(1871—1922)所说的那样,"注意力可以有多种形式,而艺术家的工作就是唤起这些形式中最好的那一种"。

21

体验与注意力

所有审美事物的共同点非常简单：你集中注意力的方式。你可能在药物诱发或性冲动（或两者皆有）的情况下集中注意力。但是，即使你凝视着一幅杰作，往往也无法集中注意力。

注意力造成的差异

还记得《007之金手指》吗？这是一部上乘的"詹姆斯·邦德"电影（1964年拍摄）。这部电影讲述的是痴迷黄金的恶棍奥里克·金手指计划炸毁位于诺克斯堡的所有联邦黄金储备。这（见图1）就是他本人。

这是一部老电影，但如果你最近或者说最近几年间观看了这部电影，你会发现这个大反派人物金手指和美国第45任总统（见图2）的长相惊人地相似。

一旦你看到了这种相似性，你就很难忽略这一点。当你看这部电影的时候，它真的让你很困惑，尤其是考虑到金手指为了使他自己的黄金储备增值而炸毁了联邦黄金储备。至少对我来 22

图1　奥里克·金手指，"詹姆斯·邦德"系列电影《007之金手指》(1964)中主要反派人物

图2　唐纳德·J.特朗普，美利坚合众国第45任总统

说，这让我对这部电影失去了很多兴趣。

关注金手指和唐纳德·J.特朗普之间的相似性，可能会产生巨大的审美差异。它能以一种显著的审美方式改变你的体验。这突出了我们所关注的艺术品特征的重要性。把注意力放在不重要的特征上，可能会且常常会破坏我们的体验。

在这个例子中，这种注意力转移引发的审美差异很可能是负面的。不过，这并非必然。

关注一个相关的特征可以完全改变你的体验，比如16世纪的勃鲁盖尔创作的一幅弗兰德山水画（见图3）。这幅画的一半是陆地风景，一半是海景，有很好的对角线构图，中间是一个农民在全神贯注地犁地。古朴典雅的日常场景，没有什么特别引人注目之处。直到你读到这个标题：《伊卡洛斯的陨落》。

什么？伊卡洛斯在哪里？我没看到有人坠落。这个农民和那个戏剧性神话事件有什么关系？你扫视图片寻找伊卡洛斯的踪迹，然后你发现他（或者至少是他的双腿，因为他刚掉进水里）就在右下角不起眼的大船下面。

我猜你现在的体验会截然不同了。虽然画布上画着伊卡洛斯双腿的那一部分在你对这幅画的体验中并非一个特别突出的特征（也许你甚至都没有看它一眼），但现在画中其他的一切事物似乎都与它有了某种联系。

也许你之前对这幅画的体验是杂乱无章的，但是对伊卡洛斯双腿的关注将整幅画连成了一个整体。（不管怎样，这似乎就是勃鲁盖尔在近五百年前想要达到的效果。）

这里还有一个例子，这次和音乐有关。在音乐中，无论你注 意低音部还是旋律，都有很大的不同。但在某些情况下，这种差

图3　老彼得·勃鲁盖尔，《伊卡洛斯的陨落》（约1555），藏于布鲁塞尔皇家美术博物馆

异甚至更为显著。约翰·塞巴斯蒂安·巴赫的《音乐的奉献》25
（1747）的第一首卡农是一首赋格式的作品，由两种乐器演奏。
但其中有一个意想不到的转折：两种乐器演奏完全相同的旋
律——一种乐器从头到尾演奏；另一种则从结尾开始反向演奏。

如果不看乐谱，很难发现这一点。然而，一旦你注意到它，
就不可能不关注这一音乐特性。这也正是巴赫创作这首曲子的
原因，他想要展示自己高超的演奏技巧。关注这一特征就可能
会产生积极的审美差异。

下面是一个不那么杰出的例子，来自情景喜剧《老爸老妈浪
漫史》（哥伦比亚广播公司，2005—2014）。这部情景喜剧共九
季，二百多集，有许多内容都关于巴尼和罗宾这对梦幻情侣复杂
的爱情故事和婚礼。最后一季基本都在讲述他们的婚礼。然而
（剧透提醒！）就在最后一集，也就是大结局的最后两分钟，节目
统筹人决定拆散这对梦幻情侣，让罗宾和泰德复合。

粉丝们非常愤怒。大结局被评为当年最糟糕的电视时刻。
这个最后的转折让许多《老爸老妈浪漫史》的铁杆粉丝烧毁了
他们所有与剧集相关的商品和纪念品，但它也实现了另一种成
功。如果你设法让自己再看一遍九季故事的所有内容，你很难
不会以非常不同的方式看待正在展开的故事。泰德和罗宾之间
的各种瞬间会更容易吸引你的注意力。你对这三个角色之间动
态的关注方式，会截然不同于你之前不知道结局会是这样时所
给予的关注。

这个技巧在故事片中已经得到广泛使用。让观众在一部电
影上多花钱的一个方法，就是让他们再观看一遍。而怀有某种 26
抱负的电影实现这一点的方式，就是在结尾处揭示一些颠覆一

切的情节；颠覆程度之大，以至于再看一遍这部电影，再次思考你现在所知的一切，都将会是一种非常不同的体验。克里斯托弗·诺兰的《记忆碎片》（2000）和《盗梦空间》（2010）就是非常著名的例子，不过，还有很多其他例子。直到最后你才知道发生了什么。而且当你第二次看这些电影时，你会以非常不同的感觉观看它们，因为你会注意到故事中截然不同的特征。

这里还有一个例子，这次不涉及艺术，而是关于我吃过的最糟糕的一顿饭。当时我妻子即将生下我们的第一个孩子。我匆忙开车送她去医院，然后又得回去拿她住院所需的许多东西。我很饿，但是很显然，我想尽快赶回来。于是，我在打包的时候把一些吃剩的中餐放进了微波炉里。食物热得太烫了，但我没有时间让它凉下来，所以我强行把它吃了下去，我的嘴因此被烫得很厉害。这不是一次很好的用餐体验。但我只用了三分钟就离开了家！

我说那是一些吃剩的中餐，但事实上那是从城里最好的中餐馆——我们前一晚在那里吃了顿美味的晚餐——打包带回的食物。虽然不能说这是我吃过的最好吃的一顿饭，但它的确是很好吃的食物。之后一天就不那么好吃了。但这两者有什么区别呢？答案很显然，注意力上存在差异。当我兴奋地把尿布和襁褓衣物塞进手提箱时，我有很多事情需要关注，但食物不在关注范围之内。

一般来说，你所关注的东西会使你的体验产生巨大的差异。它也会使你的艺术品体验产生巨大的差异。它可能会完全毁了你的体验，就像你下次再看《007之金手指》时发生的那样（很抱歉！）；或者它可以让你的体验更有意义。某些情况下，它可以让你直观感受到，即使相同的艺术品都可以因为关注点的不同而显现出不同的样子。

　　不过，注意力的问题对于任何对美学感兴趣的人来说都是极其重要的。它不仅对从事学术研究的哲学家和艺术史学家重要，而且对任何人都重要。想象一下，你正坐在博物馆里，设法理解你面前的艺术品。你应该注意什么？你面前的艺术品有许多特征，它是由一位毫无疑问想在这件艺术品中表达很多东西的艺术家创作的。你是否应该关注那些艺术家认为重要的艺术品特征？或者你应该只关注语音导览告诉你的东西？

　　当我们接触一件艺术品时，我们总是忽略它的一些特征，而将注意力集中在其他特征上。我们忽略了绘画颜料上的裂缝，把注意力集中在油画表面的其他特征上；我们将注意力从这些裂缝中抽离了出来。在看到巴洛克时期重建的罗马风格教堂时，我们可能会为了欣赏中世纪的结构而忽略巴洛克元素。同样，我们的注意力再次从艺术品的某些特征中抽离。

　　但我们如何知道应该关注艺术品的哪些特征，应该忽略哪些特征或主动不予考虑？恐怕没有简单的答案或者容易获得的捷径。注意力能够成就你的审美享受，也可以破坏它。就像《007之金手指》的例子一样，它可能是危险的；但如果（注意力）分配得当，在审美上也是非常值得的。我们应该更努力地去理解我们所关注的内容，以及我们在审美参与中如何做到这一点。

注意力焦点

　　我们从知觉心理学中了解了很多关于注意力的知识，我们也知道它会给我们的体验带来巨大的不同。近来一项十分著名的注意力实验很好地证明了这一点。你会看到一段人们打篮球的短片：一支穿白色衣服的球队对阵一支穿黑色衣服的球队。你的任务是计算第一支球队的传球次数。在这样做的同时，超过一半的实验对象没有注意到一个穿着大猩猩表演服装的人走进画面，做了一些有趣的手势，在画面里停留了整整七秒钟，然后才离开画面。如果你不是尽力地去完成所有的计数任务，你马上就会发现大猩猩。因此，你所关注的内容会对你是否在屏幕中间发现一个穿着大猩猩服装的男人产生重要的影响。这种现象有个时髦的名字："非注意盲视"。

关于这个实验，有一件很有趣的但很少被提及的事情：如果你在数另一队（即穿黑衣服的球队）的传球次数，这个实验就不成立了。其中的原因，就是大猩猩的服装是黑色的。如果你关注穿白色队服的球队，其他的一切都是干扰——不管是另一支球队、体育馆还是大猩猩服装。你对它们不予理睬，你把它们屏蔽掉了。

但是，当你关注穿黑色队服的球队时，你就会注意到大猩猩的服装，因为它也是黑色的。这并不令人感到意外。当你试图拦下一辆出租车时，你看到的每辆车要么是黄色的（或者你所在城市的出租车颜色），要么不是黄色的。那些不是黄色的车就好像根本不存在一样。它们是干扰，应该被屏蔽掉。此外，当你在漫画书《瓦尔多在哪》中寻找瓦尔多时，任何不是红色和白色条纹的东西都只是为了让你分心：你应该忽略它。

我们的大部分时间都花在关注我们所看事物的某些非常具体的特征上，而忽略了其他特征。当我们试图做一些（对注意力）要求很高的任务时，比如快速解决填字游戏，我们会尽量不去理会很多东西，这样它们就不会分散我们的注意力：我们闻到的、听到的任何东西，以及我们视野内的很多东西（除了填字游戏以外）。我们就是天生的忽略者。

如果没有这种将我们周围的世界拒之门外的神奇能力，我们会是什么样子呢？我们的大脑能力有限：如果我们想专注于某件事，我们需要忽略其他一切。大多数时候我们确实需要把注意力集中在某些事情上，比如我们的早餐、开车去上班、工作本身等等。

我们明白如何相当好地做到这一点的心理机制。即使是我们视觉处理的最初阶段也具有高度选择性：它只处理与当前时刻相关的信息。其他的信息都被放弃了。大猩猩的一些特征因为与当前任务无关而被丢弃，因为该任务只涉及穿白色衣服的球队所做的事情，因而任何黑色的东西（包括大猩猩）都变成了背景特征。

你的体验取决于你所关注的内容。如果你转移注意力，你的体验也会发生变化。在同一个音乐厅，你是在找一个空座位还是在人群中找你的朋友，决定了你的体验会非常不同。在前一种情况下，所有的人都会融化在背景中，空的座位会凸显出来。在后一种情况下，那些与你朋友面孔相似的面孔会凸显出来。这的确是非常不同的体验。

但注意力是如何描述我们的审美体验的呢？在这里，我们不仅需要讨论我们关注**什么内容**，还需要讨论我们**如何**做到这一点。关注的方式有很多种，其中一些比其他的更有助于获得（至少某种类型的）审美体验。

关注方式

　　非注意盲视研究的一个重要经验是，任何我们没有注意到的事情都不会在我们的体验中显现出来。就好像我们对它视而不见。当我们不去关注大猩猩时，我们就看不到大猩猩——我们的体验里完全没有大猩猩。因此，不关注任何事物就意味着没有任何体验。

　　如果你在一家风味美食餐厅吃了一顿美味的食物，但这顿饭是一顿重要的商务午餐——你真的需要给你的老板留下深刻印象，所以你很可能不会享受这顿饭。就用餐乐趣而言，它可能还不如平庸菜品。你的注意力转移到其他地方了，而不是在食物上。注意力是一种有限的资源：有些事情必须做出让步。

　　视觉科学家和心理学家对注意力所做的一个基本区分是，注意力可以集中或者分散。当你同时跟随屏幕上五个不同的点的轨迹时，你的注意力是分散的。如果你只跟随其中一个，你的注意力就集中了。就描述和理解所谓的视觉搜索任务（就像寻找瓦尔多这样的任务）而论，这些绝对是心理学中常见的概念。

　　这是一个关于我们会关注多少个对象的区分。但每个物体都有许多不同的特征。我的咖啡杯有颜色、形状和重量等特征。我们可以关注同一个物体，但关注的是这个物体的不同特征。关注杯子的颜色与关注它的重量会带来非常不同的体验。如果你把注意力从杯子的重量转移到杯子的颜色上，你的体验就会发生变化。所以，就像我们可以选择关注单个物体抑或关注五个物体那样，我们也可以选择关注一个物体的单个特征又或五个这样的特征。

因此,我们有四种不同的关注方式:

1. 关注单个对象的单个特征;

2. 关注多个对象的单个特征;

3. 关注多个对象的多个特征;

4. 关注单个对象的多个特征。

这种划分细致微妙且合乎逻辑,但第3项实际上并不是一个选项,这恰恰不是我们的视觉系统的构建方式。同时将我们的注意力分散到五个不同的对象上是很困难的。事实上,即使在最理想的情况下,我们也坚持不了一分钟。超过一分钟,我们的精神就会彻底耗尽。五个关注对象绝对是我们的极限:如果不是五个而是六个不同的对象,我们就无法关注其中的任何一个对象。因此,将注意力分散到不同的对象上会对资源造成一种严重的负担,即使我们跟踪的只是单个特征。如果我们试图关注多个对象的多个特征,它就不起作用了。我们最终会把一些关注对象或一些特征从我们的注意力中心弄丢。

但其他三种关注方式都很常见。就拿厨房柜台上的所有物品来说,你可以挑出其中一样东西,比如说一个咖啡杯,然后关注它的颜色。这是关注单独一个对象的唯一一个特征。你可以关注那些碰巧都是红色的物体。这是关注多个物体的唯一一个特征。而且你可以关注咖啡杯,但不需要聚焦于任何独有的特征。

每当我们执行某种精确任务时,常常会只关注单个物体的单个特征:例如,给一个苹果削皮,在这里,苹果只有一个特征是引人关注的,因而我们会忽略其他所有特征(比如,它的颜色)。关注多个对象的单个特征更为常见:比如,每次我们在寻找某种东西的时候。

当我在寻找一辆出租车的时候，我就会做这样的事。我会寻找所有这类小车的单个特征：它们是否是黄色的。奔跑着穿过机场赶飞机也涉及这种关注方式。我关注的对象很多：所有挡我路的人和行李。但对我来说，这些问题只有一个特点，即我如何绕过它们。所有其他特征都毫不相干，于是它们就被忽略了。比如，我没有注意到有多少乘客留胡子。

关注同一对象的多个特征不太常见。当你试图在风味美食餐厅享受非常昂贵的食物或者欣赏一幅画时，你关注的是单独一样东西：你吃的食物或者那件艺术品。但问题是你所关注的是食物或画的哪些特点。

因此，选择很简单：你可以全神贯注于你所看之物的唯一一个特征。有时在执行某种困难任务时这是必需的选择。但你也可以关注同一对象的多个特征。这就是很多事物引人关注的地方。

关注同一对象的多个特征并不能保证审美体验。不过，这是一个很好的切入点。当詹姆斯·邦德忙乱地试着拆除一颗定时炸弹时，他不知道哪个部分有什么功能，他关注的是单个对象的多个特征。不过，我怀疑这是否是他想要重复的体验。

我们还需要在关注同一对象的多个特征时保持自由和开放。詹姆斯·邦德所做的事情如下：他忙乱地把他无比集中的注意力从炸弹的一个部位转移到另一个部位，寻求一种让它停止的方法。他知道自己需要做什么，只是不知道如何去做。他关注很多特征，但他对所有这些特征的关注都非常敏锐。

当我们进行某种审美体验时，我们所做的恰恰与此相反：我

32

美学

们并不是在寻找任何特定的东西。我们关注眼前并不怎么罕见的场景的多个特征，但我们也没有试图专注于任何特定的特征或任何一组特征。我们的注意力是自由和开放的。

我已做了很多区分，但现在只有一个对我们来说很重要：开放式和非开放式（或者，我称之为固定式）注意力之间的区别。所有的开放式注意力都是分散的，但并不是所有分散的注意力都是开放式的，例如，詹姆斯·邦德的注意力就不是。如果我们想拥有开放式注意力，分散的注意力是一个好的开始，但这还不够。

削苹果的时候，我们的注意力是固定的（也许与专业削苹果皮的人的注意力不同，但肯定是像我这样的）。它专注于单个物体的单个特征。这就是固定和集中的注意力。当我们在找出租车的时候，我们的注意力也是固定的，只会聚焦所有汽车的单个特征：黄色。不过，邦德的注意力也是固定的，集中在炸弹的许多特征上。这就是固定的与分散的注意力。这些体验都不涉及开放式注意力，而且也没有什么乐趣。

视觉科学最初对集中的注意力和分散的注意力做出了区分。但是分散的注意力并不能保证开放性。当你在寻找出租车时，你的注意力是分散的（在不同的物体上），但根本不是开放式的。而且詹姆斯·邦德的注意力也是分散的，但不是开放式的。我把开放式注意力的标签用于这样的关注方式：我们把注意力分散到单个物体的许多特征上，但心中没有一个明确的目标或目的。

从长远来看，固定的注意力会让人疲惫不堪。开放式注意力对大脑来说是一种放松的形式，或者至少对感知系统来说是一种放松。而且我们的感知系统的确喜欢时不时地放松一下。

在这里打一个比方可能会有所帮助：健身。你可以只锻炼二头肌，着了魔似的，一遍又一遍。这相当于把你的注意力只集中在单个特征上。但你也可以同时锻炼几块肌肉，比如在跑步机上锻炼你的二头肌。这就相当于关注同一物体的多个特征。但这两种情况都与开放式注意力无关。

锻炼自然会对你有好处，但是每天都用一整天来锻炼那就太过了。你也需要放松。放松并不是说一动不动，而是，比如说，在街上悠闲地漫步，让你的许多肌肉都运动起来，但都不会过量。这就相当于开放式注意力。

一个很大的区别是：我们很少有人整天锻炼。但我们大部分时间的确都是以一种专注的方式关注着（某事）。否则就会有很多盘子掉在地上，牛奶泼洒，交通事故频发。因此，当我们不需要全神贯注的时候，我们需要对所做之事格外小心，因为这些珍贵的时刻极为罕见。

而且，就像你不锻炼任何肌肉时你的身体需要休息一样，当你的注意力不集中时，你的感知系统也需要休息。如果一出健身房就开始锻炼不同的肌肉，这完全就是傻瓜行为。当我们不需要为避免交通堵塞而全神贯注，或者不必为了不搞砸我们的晋升而更加专注时，浪费这些珍贵的时刻也是傻瓜行为。开放式注意力是大脑的休息时间，若没有它，生活将会很不幸。

我并不是说审美体验就是放松感知系统。但如果感知系统
超过承受能力，审美体验就不太可能发生。开放式注意力很特别，它可以让我们比较一幅画中两个看似不相关的形状；追踪发现小提琴旋律与钢琴旋律的对位方式；或者让我们能够注意食

物成分之间的差异或相似之处。这种关注方式至少是某些审美体验的特殊之处。

　　但不是所有的审美体验都是如此。尽管一些审美体验似乎是开放式体验，但你可能根本无法在这种描述中认识到某些自己最强烈的审美体验。你的一些强烈审美体验可能涉及固定的甚至是专注的注意力。你对所见之物并不保持超然，而是感到强烈的依恋。正如法国先锋派电影导演达尼埃尔·于伊耶（1936—2006）所说的那样，"我们希望人们在我们的电影中迷失自我。所有这些关于'保持距离'的说法都是胡扯"。我后面会谈到这些。但至少有一些典型的审美体验涉及开放式注意力。

感知的自由

　　在许多审美情境中，注意力是自由而开放的。詹姆斯·邦德为拆除炸弹而做的努力则两者都不是。他显然不能自由地去关注炸弹的任何特征——比如，如果他正在考虑剪断电线，再去关注电线之间的颜色搭配协调问题就太愚蠢了。这显然不是一个开放式过程。

　　开放式注意力和自由之间的这种关系可不仅仅是一个比喻。我们的注意力若是开放式的，我们就不会去寻找任何特定的东西。我们很高兴找到了自己所找到的东西，但并不需要完成特定的寻找任务。这并不是说我们对此不感兴趣。但我们没有任何具体需要寻找的东西。以这种开放式的方式参与解放了我们的知觉。

　　当我们在看一幅我们从未见过的画时，我们的注意力经常

36

在这幅画的许多特征之间来回转换：看这里，看那里。但我们不清楚我们要找的是什么。如果这是一次搜索，那么它就是一次没有限制、没有禁区的搜索。任何东西（或者几乎任何东西）都可能潜在地引人关注且具有相关性。

我们非常善于忽略和不理会我们所看到的几乎所有东西，以便我们能够关注重要的东西。但当我们的注意力不受限制时，我们也会让自己感到惊讶。这是一种比注意力固定时更加难以预测的状态，但正是这种缺乏可预测性使得它更有价值。

关注是一种行为，是我们醒着的时候一直在实施的行为。就像所有其他行为一样，我们有时自由地进行关注，但是有时却不那么自由。绝大部分时间里，并不是那么自由。绝大部分时间里，注意力是有禁区的。事实上，当我们的注意力固定时，绝大多数区域都是禁区。我们不关注的仅仅是一种令人分心的事物——它是禁区。

但是，如果我们的注意力是开放式的，它就可以自由地漫游。这种自由也解释了注意力在审美情境下发挥作用的许多重要特征。比如，一个不能令人接受的事实是，你不可能仅仅数到三，就能随心所欲地让你的注意力开放。为了试图削弱你注意力的焦点，让它更加开放，这种尝试行为本身就是一种固定注意力的练习，而这又与任何开放背道而驰。努力不去尝试是很难做到的。

另外，开放式注意力也需要时间。如果你匆匆忙忙，它就不太可能发生。原因很简单。当我们赶时间的时候，注意力的开放性就会受到破坏。我们无法让我们的注意力自由滚动，因为我们要在30秒内圆满完成所有的事情。

把注意力想象成黄油。这是一种有限的资源，但可以按不同的方式使用。你可以将它薄薄地或者厚厚地涂抹。如果它被 分散涂抹在许多可能会受到关注的特征上，那么它就会被涂抹得非常稀薄，每一个这样的特征就会得到更少的黄油。这些特征所得到的关注就更柔和、更温和、更不具穿透力。它更令人愉快。

审美注意力

开放式注意力是审美体验的一个重要特征。这是一个成败攸关的条件吗？不太可能。它抓住了一个特定时期（大概是在过去几百年）、世界上一个特定地区（大概就是"西方"）一种非常有影响力的审美体验形式。我们几乎没有证据表明中世纪的人是否会追求开放式注意力，而且更重要的是，在我们当前痴迷于智能手机的时代，这种关注方式可能会逐渐消失，因为痴迷智能手机时代对开放式注意力并没有多大帮助。正如先锋派行为艺术家玛丽娜·阿布拉莫维奇（1946— ）所说的那样，"如今，我们的注意力比电视广告时间还短。我们经常关注六七个问题"。这听起来完全不是开放式注意力。

像费尔南多·佩索阿、苏珊·桑塔格或者马塞尔·普鲁斯特这样的人，写了很多精彩文章讨论开放式注意力的审美体验，因此理解他们讨论的是哪种体验非常重要。但这些并不是唯一可以算作审美的一种体验。尽管如此，认真对待注意力的作用也可以帮助我们表达一些不那么开放的审美体验。

我们进行审美体验时，不只是关注我们看到的对象。我们也关注体验的质量。重要的是，我们还关注两者之间的关系。绝大部分时间里，我们关注着我们周围的事物，而没有关注我们对它们的体验。在交通堵塞时，我往往关注我前面的车，交通灯变红，挡我路的行人。

然而，我们可能还关注看见某个物体如何对我们产生影响。这意味着要关注一个物体和我们对这个物体的体验质量之间的关系。这并不意味着我们将目光投向内心，（注意力）完全被自己的体验所吸引。这个物体和我们对这个物体的体验都是我们注意力所关注的一部分，这一点很重要。

举一个很普通的例子，当我们在看一个苹果的时候，我们可以关注这个苹果的特征。或者我们可以关注我们体验这个苹果时的特征。或者我们可以同时关注两者，以及两者之间的关系。我认为第三种关注方式是审美体验的一个关键（甚至可能是普遍的）特征。

这里可以请出一种权威说法。费尔南多·佩索阿用非常相似的术语来描述审美体验。正如他所说，"真正的体验在于减少与现实的接触，同时加强对这种接触的分析"。强化对体验对象的接触分析，正是我所说的对体验对象与我们的体验质量之间的关系进行的关注。

对体验对象与我们的体验质量之间的关系进行关注，方法有很多。在本章的大部分内容中，我谈到了一种通过开放式注意力实现这一目标的具体方法，但这并不是唯一的方法。开放式和不受限制的注意力带来的一个结果是，我们的注意力可以自由转换；（注意力）不仅仅置于感知对象的特征上，而且还置于我们体验的特征上。

为第一次约会选择服装也涉及对你体验质量的关注：你停下来，看着镜子，考虑你所看到的（形象）是如何对你产生影响

美学

的。还有很多事情可能会同时发生——你可能会猜测你的约会对象会有什么反应，以及他们的反应可能与你的（反应）会有怎样的不同。但无论你做什么，它都必然涉及对体验对象和你对体验对象的体验质量之间的关系进行关注。

同样，你要花几个小时爬到山顶。你终于环顾四周。当然，你会关注这里的风景——山下的田野和河流。但不止这些。如果这就是你要做的全部所在，那么花那么多时间爬山就不值得了。你也会关注自己的体验，而这可能会受到一种成就感的影响。

达尼埃尔·于伊耶所主张的她想要激发的体验是一种专注，而不是一种开放或超脱，该如何看待？专注并不意味着我们对全神贯注于事物的体验不涉其中。当我们全神贯注的时候，我们常常会意识到我们受到了吸引——我们享受的不仅仅是吸引我们注意力的东西，也在享受全神贯注的体验本身。因此，这是另一种关注，是对我们感知之物与我们对感知之物的体验之间关系的关注。

虽然开放式注意力在审美体验中的重要性可能是一种"西方"特定的事物，但对感知对象与体验该对象的体验质量之间关系的关注，则是一个可以在许多非西方美学传统中找到的主题。一个非常明显的例子就是"拉莎"，即梵文美学的核心概念，它不仅影响了印度人的艺术思维，而且也影响了印度尼西亚人，甚至东非部分地区的人。

"拉莎"常被解释为对我们体验的情感味道所进行的品味。味道在这里不仅仅是一个比喻——在这种传统中，艺术体验是一种处理我们所有感官通道的多模态体验。但我们各种目标的关键点就是"品味"这一概念。品味一顿饭意味着你要关注不同体验的差异与和谐之间的关系。这意味着要关注不同口味是如何对你产生影响的。在强行吃下中餐剩菜的例子中，这一点正是我们没有讨论到的。"拉莎"理论把我所说的审美注意力看作我们体验艺术品过程中最重要的一个组成部分。

但有人可能会问，这是否会让审美体验变得太廉价了：我可以在拔智齿的时候关注我的体验质量。我的确可以。我还能关注到牙齿和疼痛之间的关系。但这并不能让这种体验成为一种审美体验（唉！）。我们还需要的是这种注意力的开放性。

我们现在可以把那些关于是什么让审美体验具有美感的拼图拼在一起了：我们运用注意力的方式。这是一种特殊的注意力运用，可以被描述为看见事物的美。注意力可以（但不一定）受情绪调节。

我们从"为其自身原因"理论对超然和开放性在美学领域的重要性的描述中吸取教训，因而我们可以按照几乎不带禁区的自由和开放式注意力来公平对待这一点。而且我们已经看到，愉悦描述缺乏一个审美注意力理论，而这正是我想要在这里提出的观点。

最后，该回到性、药物和摇滚的问题上了。对许多性体验来说，我们关注的是我们的感知和我们的体验质量之间的关系；而药物（体验）也是如此（赫胥黎对其服用佩奥特仙人掌后思维之旅的生动描述全是关于这方面的内容）。因此，我们没有理由否认来自这些体验的审美标签。

在古老而且到现在都有点陈腐的知觉讨论中，一个反复出现的主题是：知觉是透明的。这可能意味着我们就像通过一扇干净的窗户看东西一样看透我们的体验。一个经典的说法是，如果你盯着一个番茄看，并试图关注你对番茄的体验，那么你就会自动开始关注番茄本身。所以体验本身是透明的——你可以透过它看（事物）。

当你看到一个西红柿是因为你想吃它的时候，情况可能是这样的，也可能并非如此。我的观点是，当涉及对番茄的审美体验时，情况就截然不同了。在这种情况下，你不仅关注番茄，还关注你对番茄的体验质量，以及两者之间的关系。审美体验不是透明的。

42

美学与自我

为什么我们要花很多钱去听一场音乐会或买一本书？为什么我们要花好几个小时做一顿美食？为什么我们要花费很大力气去爬到山顶？我的答案是，我们做这些事情是为了获得对我们个人来说很重要的体验。这些体验对我们是谁以及我们认为自己是谁很重要。

有多重要呢？最近的一些实验研究表明，我们大多数人认为自己对音乐和电影的品位是我们最基本的特征之一。我们在衣食方面的品位也同样重要。想象一下，你明天醒来时，发现自己比现在聪明多了，或者更不聪明了，你是否还是你呢？或者想象一下，你一觉醒来变得更善良了，更瘦了，或者成为一个共和党人，或者对瑜伽不太感兴趣了，你是否还是你呢？

根据研究结果，上述场景中极少有场景能与以下场景相比：当你醒来，你的音乐品位与过去完全相反了。相比我们的道德、政治甚至宗教观点，我们往往认为我们的音乐品位是我们身份中更重要的组成部分。

43

改变自我，改变美学

我们对音乐、电影和艺术的品位对我们来说非常重要。不仅如此，还有我们吃什么食物、喝什么咖啡、穿什么衣服的品位。我们把自己的审美偏好看作我们身份的重要组成部分。

但这些偏好变化极快，出人意料，而且常常在我们没有注意到的情况下发生改变。根据最近的一些研究结果，审美偏好在中年人群中是最稳定的，而在年轻人和（有点出人意料的是）老年人群中则更加不稳定。但即使是最稳定的年龄组，在他们真正关心的审美领域，他们的审美偏好也至少每两周发生一次重大变化。

我们总认为自己变化不大。或者如果我们发生了变化，我们也能控制这种变化。可是，我们在这一点上大错特错。我们几乎无法控制自己的改变方式和改变的幅度。

以一个广泛探讨的心理现象——"纯粹接触效应"为例。你接触到某物的机会越多，你往往就越喜欢它。只是纯粹接触一些东西就会改变你的偏好。而且，即使你没意识到自己接触了什么，这种情况也会发生。

纯粹接触效应会影响你对人、歌曲、颜色甚至画作的喜好。在一项实验中，康奈尔大学的一位心理学教授在视觉科学导论课的幻灯片里放了一些看似随机的图片。这样一来，在关于视觉如何工作的课程中，学生们就会突然看到雷诺阿或莫里索的画，且没有任何图解说明。它只是作为点缀出现。

虽然这些画似乎是随机出现的，但它们是实验的一部分。44
一些图片要比其他图片出现的频率更高；在学期末，学生们被要求对所展示的图片进行打分。学生们给那些出现次数更多的图片打的分，系统性地比那些只出现一次的图片打分要高。这些学生中几乎没有人说他们还记得以前看过这些图片。

即使你没有意识到这种接触，也会产生纯粹接触效应。关于纯粹接触效应的一组重要发现是，即使是无意识的接触也会增加积极评价的可能性，比如刺激物只闪过很短时间（不到200毫秒）或者刺激物被掩饰（即巧妙隐藏）的情况。这些发现很难不让人感到些许不安。我们可以控制自己所接触的音乐和艺术类型，但绝对无法完全控制。找到一个没有音乐的公共空间越来越难。咖啡馆、购物中心、电梯，你在这些地方接触到的音乐会在你的喜好上留下印记，但这种情况极少会是让我们满意之事。

我们在音乐、电影、食物、服装和艺术方面的审美偏好对我们来说极其重要，这些偏好能够而且确实会以一种我们无法控制的方式发生变化。如果你是自由爵士乐的粉丝，而且你认为自己具有自由爵士乐风格，那么在超市里听到贾斯汀·比伯的音乐会让你更加喜欢他特定的音乐风格一点。你很可能对此毫无察觉。它在未被注意到的情况下悄然发生。

如果我们的偏好可以在我们没有注意到的情况下被强行控制，那么我们身份的很大部分似乎都是随机纯粹接触的产物。我们对此毫无防御能力。在我年轻且自命不凡的时候，我总是闭着眼睛走过博物馆的流行艺术展厅。但要做到这一点是有困难的（还有一点危险）。而且涉及音乐时，就更困难了。我们的品位会改变，我们对此却无能为力。发现这种令人不安的情况非常容易，这一事实表明审美领域对自我是多么重要。但我们

45

也不能忽视美学与自我之间的紧密联系。

体验与评价

"西方"美学大多是关于见多识广的审美判断。审美判断是
一种（通常只对你自己但有时也对别人所做的）状态说明：某个
特定的对象是美丽的、优雅的、丑陋的或恶心的。但我们绝大多
数的审美参与并非如此。如果是这样的话，我们就很难解释为
什么我们如此在意一切美的事物了。我们看一部三小时的电影
或者在山上远足一天的原因，并不是为了对电影或风景做出充
分的审美判断。如果我们严肃地看待美学在我们生活中的重要
性，那么我们就需要将重点从审美判断转移到各种审美参与形
式上——这更令人愉快、更加有益，而且更为频繁地发生在我们
身上。

我们不会为了发表审美判断意见而去听音乐会或烹饪几个
小时。我们很难理解为什么审美判断对我们如此重要。做出审
美判断真的没有那么有趣，也不是特别有价值。如果我们的确
在做出审美判断中获得某种乐趣（比如，我们为自己最喜欢的五
本书或电影排名，并将其发布到社交媒体上），这种乐趣可能更
多地与这种评价的交流有关，而不是在于真正做出的评价。在
电影院看完一部电影后，你和朋友就这部电影展开长时间激烈
的辩论也是如此。

相比之下，我们在审美环境中随时间展开的体验是有趣的、
有益的，也是我们个人所关心的。它有时会但并非永远都在审
美判断中达到它的终点，然而这不是我们这么做的原因所在。
专注于体验而不是评价判断的一个主要优势是，它可以帮助我

们理解"为自我而美"的所有事物的个体重要性和紧迫性。

但什么是审美判断呢？你去博物馆，然后盯着一幅画看。你坐在它前面，盯着它看了二十分钟。然后你站起来，就对它形成了一种审美判断。然后，你可以把你的审美判断与你的朋友交流或发在博客上。你对这幅画的体验持续了二十分钟。做出评价通常发生在这个过程的最后（当然，你可以在这个过程中做出评价，可能会在以后对它进行修改）。西方美学主要关注的是这个过程最后的评价，而不是这二十分钟体验的时间演进（包括注意力的转移、视觉比较等）。

审美判断甚至不会发生在我们每一次的审美接触中。这是一种可选特性。假设我在这幅画前花了二十分钟，但是我不能确定它的美学优点和缺点，我可以暂缓做出评价。这并不会让我对该艺术品的审美参与变得不那么值得或者不那么有意义，又或少了乐趣。事实上，它有时会让你的体验更加愉快。

关于审美判断与其他类型评价的不同之处，已有很多讨论。根据广义的康德哲学观点，审美判断可能不仅仅是体验的终点；它可能贯穿整个过程，并对我们的体验本身产生影响。但是，即使在这个看起来更以体验为中心的背景下，最重要的还是评价。只要我们做出正确的评价，它就能引导我们获得正确的体验。正如我们在第三章中多次看到的那样，注意力可以从根本上改变我们的体验。但审美判断却很少能做到。仅仅因为我相信这幅画是美丽的或优雅的，我对它的体验就不太可能发生变化（更不用说变得更好了）。相比之下，关注各种各样到现在为止都未注意到的特征，可以显著地改变我的体验。

如果我们认为美学应该主要关注我们对艺术品的体验如何

在时间上展开（无论这种时间的展开是否以审美判断为终点），那么这种以审美判断为起点的总体描述就是错误的。我们不应承认这种假设的成立：仅仅因为所有事物都是审美判断的组成要素，就肯定地认为我们用这些要素所组建的所用东西都是美的。我们应该凭自身力量检验我们的审美参与或审美体验，而不是从审美判断领域借用任何概念性工具。

我们青春期的审美体验

这里有一场引人注目的论证，说明美学的重要性与我们见多识广的审美判断几乎没有什么关系。还记得你第一次强烈的审美体验吗？你那时是一个孩子还是一个青少年？是某些音乐让你神魂颠倒，还是某处风景令你屏息敛气？下面是我个人生活中的三个例子，你可以把这些例子换成你年轻时的例子。

证据一：我那时十六岁，站在老的泰特美术馆里（当时还没有泰特现代美术馆），被一幅克利福德·斯蒂尔（1904—1980）的油画迷住了。我当时可能在那里待了两个小时。我当时对克利福德·斯蒂尔还不太了解。我知道他是一个抽象表现主义者，但仅此而已。我非常喜欢这幅画，所以第二天——我本应该和我的高中同学一起参观伦敦塔和国会大厦，我却离开了他们，回到皮姆利科再看一看（这幅画）。

证据二：时间倒回一年。米开朗基罗·安东尼奥尼的电影《放大》（1966）让我如此着迷，以至于我一周去电影院看两三次。我把整部电影的对白都背下来了。每一次，我都在一种狂喜的状态下离开电影院，因为我理解了关于爱情、外表和现实以及其他深层次问题等一些真正重要的东西。

证据三：时间再倒回一年。我读了一本令我震撼的书：鲍里斯·维安的《泡沫人生》（1947）。我以前从未有过这种感觉：我一时间既想哭又想笑。

我想表达的观点是：我现在认为《放大》是安东尼奥尼最糟糕的一部电影。《泡沫人生》提到的很多事情都是我十四岁时不可能理解的，而且比起维安的其他一些小说，它的原创性大打折扣。我现在仍然认为克利福德·斯蒂尔是了不起的，但在那批收藏品中另有许多伟大的艺术作品，出于某种原因，我却喜欢上了这幅画。

为写本章内容做准备，我昨天去了泰特现代美术馆，看看我对那幅画是否有反应。还好，不是很强烈。我也看了一遍《放大》（因为电影院似乎不再放映安东尼奥尼的电影了，所以用笔记本电脑观看），但看了二十分钟左右就不得不关机，实在受不了。我看了几页英语译本的《泡沫人生》后便放下了（公平地说，这是因为翻译的缘故）。

当我第一次接触这些艺术品时，我对它们有着更强烈、更有益的审美体验；相比现在，我那时对艺术史、电影史或20世纪法国文学史了解甚少，我现在了解得多一点。我想，相比我十四岁至十六岁的时候，我现在能更好地评估这些作品的美学价值。我现在可以做出一种更好的审美判断了。但现在不像当时那样充满热情。

以我的后见之明，我应该谴责十四岁到十六岁的本斯的审美判断，不是吗？但是，如果我那时没对这些作品产生如此强烈的感觉，我可能就不会对艺术产生兴趣，也就不会学到所有这些知识——让我现在能以高人一等的态度对待少年的本斯。

49

什么是见多识广的审美判断呢？就拿我刚才对《放大》所做的评价来说，它是安东尼奥尼最糟糕的一部电影。我们被告知，这就是美学应该做出的判断。十五岁的我对《放大》的喜爱并不是美学的内容。

我的例证旨在表明，在审美判断的成熟度和我们审美体验的强度之间，可能存在而且经常存在着不匹配。由此可得出一个结论：如果只关注见多识广的审美判断，就会将一些真正重要的东西排除在美学讨论之外——审美参与是令人愉快的，而且它对我们来说具有一定的个体重要性。我们关注审美参与。片面地关注见多识广的审美判断，就无法公正地对待这个非常简单的美学事实。

体验至上

我介绍这些例子还有一个更重要的原因。我们已经看到，并不是我们的审美判断越可靠，我们的审美体验就越强烈或越有价值。这样做的一个结果是，我们应该将这些强烈的、有益的和对个人很重要的美学体验纳入美学讨论，而不是为了专注于美学判断而牺牲这些体验。但在一个完全不同的意义上，体验也是先于评价的。我们每一个见多识广的审美判断都依赖于一些早期的体验——这些体验是有益的，对我们个人来说很重要，但根本不是见多识广的知识。

当你走进博物馆里一个有许多画作的展厅，快速地环顾四周，也许你会喜欢上其中一些展出的画作，但不喜欢其他的画作。你不知道哪幅画是谁画的，因此，进行任何有根据的评价都是不可能的。但正是这种最初的喜好决定了你会接近哪一幅画，并花更多的时间去探索。我们能够对所有的事物做出可靠的审美判断，唯一的原因就是我们在几秒钟前或者几十年前就喜欢上了一些艺术品，这就是我们现在对这件艺术品而不是其他艺术品进行（审美）接触的原因所在。

让我们后退一步。我们这里有两个审美参与的例子，即我十几岁时的体验（非常积极、非常有价值、对我个人来说非常重要）以及我现在做出的这个评价（认为这件作品有点平庸、不怎么有价值、对我个人来说不重要）。后者就是我们所说的见多识广的审美判断。但如果没有前者，后者也不可能发生。这里就存在一个问题：如何解释早期的审美参与所带来的审美愉悦？如果我们把讨论局限在审美判断上，就很难弄明白我们应该如何回答这个问题。这不可能是我们成熟的审美判断，因为早期的审美判断根本不成熟或者不可靠。这种强烈且有益的早期体验也许是完全不充分且与审美无关的，但不充分且与审美无关的反应似乎在很大程度上决定了我们的审美偏好，就像我目前的审美偏好很大程度上就是青少年本斯审美体验的产物一样。

这可不是一个微不足道的小问题。这里有一个让它变得更紧迫的方法：如果我对自己的审美判断不感兴趣，那我为什么还要在乎它们呢？它们既没有给我带来任何快乐，对我个人也没有任何重要性。如果学习的结果是我们对接触艺术品的兴趣减少，我们为什么还要学习更多的艺术史和20世纪法国文学史呢？

这里有一个解决这个难题的办法。审美判断并不是那么有趣。不管是我十几岁时做的那种天真的评价，还是我现在做的那种见多识广的评价，都不那么有趣。总体来看，进行评价很少是有益的、有趣的或令人愉快的。而另一方面，体验可以是非常

51

有益的、有趣的或令人愉快的。同样，做出评价很少会成为我们觉得具有个人意义的事情。体验是我们觉得有意义的东西。因此，美学应该讨论体验，而不是评价。这些体验能够产生可与他人交流的评价，这是一种很好的附加物，不过体验未必就引发评价。

我们花这么多时间和金钱去接触艺术品，并非因为我们想对它们做出审美判断。我们这样做是因为我们在接触艺术品时所获得的体验是愉快的、有价值的、对个人有意义的。不是判断，而是经验（才是如此）。

我们应该努力摆脱审美判断的概念，不管它是否可靠。与艺术品进行审美接触的目的极少是要提出审美判断；我们的审美理论应该尊重这一事实。我们应该关注我们审美体验的时间演进，而不是（很显然属于任选的）宣布审美判断的终点行为。正如苏珊·桑塔格所说的那样："将一件艺术品作为艺术品来接触是一种体验，而不是一个观点陈述或者对一个问题的回答。"

为何要判断？

为了将美学理论的重点从审美判断转移到审美参与的时间演进上，我们需要理解为什么美学家一开始就痴迷于审美判断。　52

其中一个原因显然是历史原因。西方美学的核心概念一直是审美判断，至少从二百五十多年前大卫·休谟（1711—1776）出版《品味标准》（1757）开始就是如此。

休谟对英美哲学美学的影响不容忽视，他明确地谈到了两个不同的人判断品味的方法差异。他给出了下面的故事作为例证（借用《堂吉诃德》里的故事）。两个人喝了同一种酒，并被要求对酒的品质进行评价。其中一人说，它有一种可分辨出来的奇怪的皮革味。另一个认为它有一种难闻的金属气味。休谟的故事妙就妙在，我们可能会认为这些评价中至少有一个是完全错误的，但在检查葡萄酒时，他们发现了一个小钥匙，上面系着一个小皮圈。所以他们都是对的。

我会在第五章再回到这个故事上。但现在对我们来说很重要的是，虽然休谟在这里明确强调了感知辨别的重要性，但他主要关心的是这两位品酒师的审美判断。对他们来说，他们对葡萄酒的体验是如何随着时间的推移而展开的并不重要（不过，关于葡萄酒的体验是如何随着时间的推移而展开的，有很多内容可讲）。唯一重要的是他们提出的审美判断——以及这两种评价之间的关系如何。

我们将在第五章中看到，休谟关注判断有重要的哲学原因，但他在美学领域的强大影响力意味着他的假设——美学的中心关注点是理解审美判断——是毫无争议的。

审美判断在美学中占主导地位的另一个重要历史原因，与语言哲学对一般哲学尤其是对美学的强烈影响有关。审美判断是一种（我们对自己或对他人所做出的）状态说明，语言哲学对此有很大的发言权。因此，对于具有浓厚语言哲学修养的美学家来说，审美判断是一个熟悉的主题。相比之下，用语言哲学的概念工具来分析体验就不那么容易了。

走向全球

如果把我们所认为的美学范围从严格的"西方"美学扩大到全球美学，我们就不难发现这种以判断为中心的观点的特点。

"西方"以外的绝大多数美学传统根本就不太关心审美判断。他们关注的是我们的情感如何呈现，我们的感知如何发生改变，以及审美参与如何与社会参与相互作用。

最极端的例子来自伊斯兰美学（尤其是苏菲派传统的伊斯兰美学）。伊斯兰美学与"西方"美学传统的一个不同之处在于，它强调世界整体上不断变化的特征，尤其是我们对艺术品的体验。艺术接触的特殊之处在于我们对这些不断变化、闪烁不定的体验的感受（比如，当我们在某些建筑周围移动时，某些建筑特征会刻意提供给我们不同的景致，它们在水中一闪而过的倒影往往进一步强调了这一点）。这一传统非常感兴趣的是美，而不是对美的判断；它对利用我们感知系统的工作方式来解释美的方法感兴趣。它强调我们体验中不断变化、闪烁不定的特征，使得任何企图做出固定评价的努力都成了不可能。

我们也看到了"拉莎"理论如何讨论我们多模态情感体验的品味，而不是判断——"拉莎"理论几乎就没有讨论过它。在极少数情况下，我们所说的审美判断在"拉莎"理论中被提到时，就是为了表明，固定而不灵活的判断实际上是如何与我们的体验品味**背道而驰的**。最后，举一个有点模糊的例子，在亚述-巴比伦美学中，"塔布里图"的关键概念通常被翻译为仰慕和敬畏，但它被非常清楚地认定为对艺术品的感性体验，这涉及"反复和持续不断"的观察——再一次说明，这是逐步展开的体验，而不是判断。审美判断在我们西方传统中扮演如此重要的角色，这一事实不过是历史上的一种罕见之物罢了。

为什么审美判断的概念在"西方"美学中占主导地位，一个历史意义不大但更有实质意义的原因是，审美判断是可以交流传播的。当我们产生审美分歧时，我们是在审美判断上有分歧：我说电影不好，你则说它很好。因此，为了理解我们对艺术品审美接触的主体间性和社会性，这种争论会继续下去，我们需要关注审美判断。第五章的主题就是美学的这种人际维度。

55

第五章

美学与他者

美学很少是一项孤立的尝试。我们一起吃饭，和朋友一起去博物馆，一起为我们的公寓挑选家具。当我们去听音乐会或看电影时，我们所在的大厅里满是与我们有着相似体验的人。我们是社会人，因而极少存在缺乏各种社会性的审美情境。

此外，如果两个朋友在听同一首歌时有相似的体验，这可能是他们之间一个重要的联系。如果你们观看同一部电影时，你的朋友拥有的是一段非常糟糕的体验，而你却有一段令人兴奋的体验，那么这就会让人产生疏远感。

审美的一致与分歧

略微令人遗憾的是，"西方"美学史上关于美学社会维度的讨论，一直都只被一个问题主导着：审美的一致与分歧问题。

谁是更好的作曲家，约翰尼·罗顿还是沃尔夫冈·阿玛多伊斯·莫扎特？喷涌而出的直觉告诉你，莫扎特更好，大家都知道这一点。审美在这一点上达成了完全的一致。如果还没有 56

（达成审美一致性），就应该（达成一致）。那些喜欢约翰尼·罗顿的人本应更清楚这一点。他们应该多听听莫扎特的音乐，这样他们就会认识到自己观点的错误。

在某种意义上，把约翰尼·罗顿和莫扎特进行比较是愚蠢的。可能极少会发生这样激烈的深夜争论：一个人（严肃地）支持约翰尼·罗顿，而另一个人则为莫扎特辩护。但实际上，我们确实经常争论许多审美问题，这是我们争论的最重要的事项之一。巴赫更好还是亨德尔更好？弗里达·卡罗还是迭戈·里维拉？或者，如果这些争论似乎太过高雅，那么披头士更好还是滚石乐队更好？《宋飞正传》更好还是《发展受阻》更好？哪一部《速度与激情》更好？还可以抛开艺术不谈：（《星球大战》中的人物）汉·索罗和"天行者"卢克哪个更有吸引力？巴黎比巴塞罗那更漂亮吗？咖啡豆要深烘焙好还是浅烘焙更好？牛排三分熟还是五分熟比较好？诸如此类，不一而足。

这里有公认的两个解决这类分歧的选项。我们可以求同存异。你喜欢这个，我喜欢那个。我们俩都不对，或者相反地，我们俩都对。另一种选项是，我们中的一个完全错了。这两个选项的合理性将取决于我们选择的例子。把约翰尼·罗顿和莫扎特进行对比的案例，是支持第二种选项的一个卑鄙之举。而选择弗里达·卡罗还是迭戈·里维拉的例子可以被视为对第一种选项的支持。

请比较一下审美上的分歧与在那些不具美感的事物上所产生的分歧。如果我们都在看一幅画，我说它是方形的，而你说它是三角形的，那么至少有一个人是错误的。但是，如果我们都看着同一幅画，但对它的审美品质存在不同意见，事情就没那么清晰明确了。

另一种对比可能会带有明显的"主观"分歧。如果我们看
着同一幅画，我说它让我想起了我的祖母，而你说它没有让你想
起你的祖母，那么这两种观点相互一致（即使我们有同一个祖
母）。我是对的，而你也是对的。

现在的问题是，审美上的分歧是更接近于"正方形与三角
形"的分歧，还是更接近"是否让我想起我的祖母"的分歧。"西
方"美学中一些最重要的教科书都试图在纯粹"主观的"分歧
（比如涉及我的祖母的那个分歧）和纯粹"客观的"分歧（比如
涉及形状的那个分歧）之间创造出一个中间状态。

还记得休谟所说的带皮圈的铁钥匙的故事吗？他之所以
举出这个寓言故事作例证，正是为了解决审美的一致性与分歧
问题。那两位品酒专家意见不同，一个分辨出铁的味道，另一个
分辨出皮革的味道。但事实证明两者都是正确的。他们都是对
的，但并不是因为味觉评判完全是"主观的"，而是因为他们的
味觉评判有一个"客观的"基础：带皮圈的钥匙。但如果有第三
位专家加入进来，说葡萄酒尝起来像硫黄，那她就错了。味觉的
判断比那些让我想起祖母的东西的判断更受限制，但没有形状
的判断那么受限。

美学并非用于监管

在审美分歧争论这一点上，一个冗长而让人感到怀疑的词
总是出现：规范性。这种观点认为，审美评价具有某种规范效
力。在欣赏某种事物时，我们应该做出某种判断。如果我们不
做出这类判断，我们就错了：我们没有做我们应该做的事情。

一般认为美学领域在这方面与道德领域相似：两者都是关于我们应该做什么，而不是我们实际上做了什么。伦理学告诉我们，我们是否应该撒谎、偷窃或成为素食者。美学告诉我们应该有什么样的审美体验，以及该在什么时候体验。

规范性就是关于我们应该做什么事情。我们审美生活的许多特征在某些方面就非常具有规范性。我本人曾提出一个相当具有规范性的主张，即美学不应给予"西方"特权，并且我会一直如此主张。而且，若没有提出至少某些规范性主张就很难谈论一些得到确认的审美实践，例如，一首音乐作品的表演者**应该**做什么，才能算作对该音乐作品（而不只是随机的音符）的一种表演。当我们谈论审美领域时，"应该"这个词会随处出现（而且在本书中也会层出不穷）。

尽管如此，美学并不是一门规范性学科，这一点我再怎么强调也不为过。伦理学的某些内容可能真的与规范性主张有关（伦理学的一个分支被称为"规范性伦理学"，所以这是个不错的候选项）。但美学不是。美学主要不是讨论我们应该做什么，它是讨论我们在什么样的环境下实际做了些什么。

你可能期望伦理学的某部作品能说服你应该成为素食者还是继续吃肉。但你不应指望任何美学作品会给你提出这样的建议。美学不会试图告诉你应该做什么——应该欣赏哪些艺术作品，应该忽略哪些。这种美学思维方式还要走很长的一段路，才能驱散许多艺术家对美学作为一门学科的那种强烈的不信任感——这些艺术家常常认为美学正在告诉他们什么是被允许做的，什么是不被允许做的，而且更重要的是，对他们的作品该做出什么样的反应才是恰当的。

伦理学的某些分支可能是关于在道德问题上对你的行为进行监管，但是美学并不是要监管你的审美反应。你的审美反应就是审美反应，而且你也不应该让任何人来对它们进行监管。因此，我们应该以高度怀疑的眼光看待美学中出现的任何像"规范性"这样的词语。

而且，这也适用于审美分歧争论中出现的"规范性"之类的词语。人们普遍认为，审美判断或审美评价具有规范性效力。这可能意味着很多事情。这可能意味着你的审美反应可能是正确的，也可能是错误的。如果你喜欢上不受人喜欢的作品，那你就错了。如果你不喜欢大师级作品，那你又错了。在面对某一作品时，你**应该**有一定的情感或审美反应。如果你不这样做，你的审美反应就不是它应该有的样子。你有这种反应是**不对的**。

如果你不喜欢这种关于审美思路的专制口吻，那么你必须意识到，这个背景深深植根于一种非常特殊（而且完全以"西方"为中心）的美学思维方式。很容易看出我们如何对审美判断做出规范性主张。判断可能是对的，也可能是错的；但它们常常是错误的。不过，如果我们感兴趣的是经验，而不是判断，那我们又怎么会形成规范性主张呢？以下是一个尝试。虽然体验不可能是正确的或错误的，但它们可以是准确的或不准确的。例如，感知错觉是不准确的。就像你可能会因为天色太过昏暗而看错物体的颜色一样，你也可能会有一种错觉的审美体验。

至关重要的是，这一论点只有在我们认同用我所谓的美容院方法讨论美学时才成立，即这样一种观点：让体验具有美感的是，它与美的事物有关，并且美的事物与不美的事物之间存在着一条严格的分割线。当我们有一种不准确的审美体验时，我们

60

就会把美的事物体验为不美的事物（或者把不美的事物体验为美的事物）。

不过我们已经知道了，美学的美容院方法未必就是一种吸引人的观点。让体验具有美感的并不是体验一种美的事物，使它具有美感的是你运用注意力的方式。而且，运用注意力的方式不存在准确或不准确。因此，尽管体验可能是准确的或虚幻的，但让它们具有美感的却与它们的准确性无关。它与运用注意力的方式息息相关。

让我们回到审美分歧的争论上。这个问题是：审美分歧更像是讨论油画形状的分歧（你说是三角形，我说是正方形），还是更像讨论这幅画是否让我想起我的祖母的分歧？不过，只要提出这个问题，也就认为美容院方法研究美学是理所当然的。

如果对审美参与很重要的东西却与被感知对象的特征没有什么关系，那么对于其他特征（比如形状以及它是否让我想起我的祖母等）上的分歧进行比较就没有意义了。

当你和我看着同一件艺术品或相同风景时，我的体验可能与你的体验截然不同。但是，将这种差异定义为一种分歧，要么是偷偷强调审美判断（而不是体验），要么是把我们整个交给美容院方法。

如果你和我在同一件艺术品或风景前有不同的体验，这对我们来说很重要。这比不同形状或什么东西让谁想起祖母的争论更加重要。而且，将审美参与的社会维度简化为审美分歧，并不能理解美学在我们日常生活和日常社会交往中的重要性。

下面来看一个有点尴尬的例子。比如，如果我们倾向于和那些喜欢相同音乐的人在一起厮混，并且鄙视那些喜欢不同音

61

乐的人,那么审美的社会维度似乎就特别重要。当我在高中的时候(我是一个非常自命不凡的人,正如我们在第四章看到的那样),我花了一个夏天在德国,据说是学习德语。我非常喜欢其中一个德国女孩,而且她也非常喜欢我;在多次远足游玩后,我们之间萌动的感情就把我们带去了她的住所。我记得我看到的第一样东西就是一张艾罗斯·拉玛佐第的巨幅海报,因为她是这位意大利流行歌手的粉丝。

一个明显的审美分歧就摆在那——这么说吧,我不是艾罗斯·拉玛佐第的粉丝。但我还是从短暂的变故中挺过来了。这时,为了营造浪漫的气氛,她把灯光调暗,放了一张艾罗斯·拉玛佐第的激光唱片。在审美问题上有意见分歧是可以的,但当被迫分享对艾罗斯·拉马佐蒂音色的浪漫体验时,那就太过分了。

审美上的分歧很重要,这是毫无疑问的;但分享或未能成功分享审美体验更为重要。而且,审美体验的方式没有对错之分。

但这并不意味着任何东西都要装进美学之中。有些艺术品显然试图唤起非常特定的反应;如果你有相反的反应,那么就偏离了方向。假设你正坐在博物馆里你最喜欢的一幅画前,你没有体验到你认为在博物馆的这幅画前能够或者在某种意义上应该体验到的东西。从某种重要意义上说,你是失败的,但这并不是某种需要加以监管的失败。

正如我们所看到的那样,我们可以通过将某人的注意力吸引到某些特征上来改变她的审美体验。与严厉打击异常体验相比,这是一种更好的处理体验差异的方式。缺乏监管不会导致混乱状态。如果幸运的话,它会带来对话、和平共处和多样性。

再回到规范性以及对它的滥用上。对规范性的一种更温和

62

但危害丝毫不减的诉求，就是对审美评价的普遍诉求。这并不是说某一种艺术作品只要求你有特定的审美反应。相反地，当你产生审美反应时，你会完全假设其他人都有或者至少应该有相同的反应。这是康德的观点，因此已对"西方"美学产生了深远的影响。

我试图保持委婉的态度，而且对康德哲学的思想成就心感敬畏，但这无疑是美学史上最傲慢的一种思想。如果你完全假设其他人应该和你有同样的反应，那么你就严重低估了人类的多样性以及人们出生的文化背景的多样性。每当我们受到诱导而认为（或假设或意识到）我们所做的任何事情都具有普遍的吸引力或普遍的沟通性时，那将会是一个很好的时机，停下来，去运用我所谓的"审美谦逊"思考一下，与这个星球上巨大的文化多样性相比，我们自己的地位和文化背景是多么偶然。我将在第七章再讨论这些主题。

现实生活中的审美分歧

关于审美一致性与分歧的真正问题并不是谁对谁错。它是关于我们的体验如何依赖于我们的注意力分配、我们的背景观念和知识以及我们过去的接触。理解这些因素能够怎样改变我们的体验，可以极大地帮助我们解决审美分歧。

我曾经当过电影评论家。这份工作的好处之一就是可以参加电影节，我常常是电影节评委之一。成为电影节的评委有其令人向往的一面——会见著名的男女电影明星，住在高级酒店，等等。但有时这也是一种令人精疲力竭而且常常令人愤怒的体验。

63

你和另外四名来自世界不同地区的评委坐在一起，而且他们对电影的品位和你的截然不同，但你需要决定哪部电影应该获奖，而且做出这样的决定总是有一个严格的期限。你必须在午夜前给音乐节的组织者一个电影名，现在已经是晚上十一点了，还没有就（推荐）哪一部电影达成一致。这是现实生活中的审美分歧，而解决这个分歧的任务连休谟也未必能帮上忙。在担任过几次评委后，关于审美分歧的陈腐辩论在我看来开始变得迥然不同了。

这些评委会议的目的不是分享体验，而是进行严格的审美判断。我们必须达成一致意见：某部电影比其他的更好。事实上，它的工作方式通常是相反的。首先，我们得达成一致意见：有些电影显然不会获奖。这是比较容易的部分。但到后来我们只剩下四五部电影的时候，就需要进行动真格的评选。

你有方法理性地说服另一位电影评论家，她喜欢的电影实际上是模仿之作且毫无新意吗？恐怕答案是"没有而且也不能"。这种争论毫无理性可言。而且令人悲哀的是，这个奖项常常会颁给一部没有令任何一位电影评论家着迷，却能让我们所有人都接受其获奖的电影。

这种说服不是理性的——而且我很少看到电影评论家试图保持理性。（一些更有经验的电影评论家还会尝试某种形式的心理战，在评委会讨论之前，通常是在放映期间，系统性地削弱某些电影的地位，有时是无意识地事先做好不利于这些电影的铺垫。这种心理战也不是理性的，而是在更情绪化的层面上进行的。不过，我不确定的是，除了评论家们的狡诈之外，对一般美学来说，还能从中学到什么……）

在这些评委身上发生的几乎唯一一件事，就是试图让其他电影评论家关注这些电影的某些特征。这并不像在评判油画或小说时那么明显，因为电影是一种时间艺术。我们在看过这些电影的几天后所能关注的不是电影本身，而是我们对电影的回忆。

尽管如此，几乎所有的争论实际上都是把其他评论家的注意力引向一些迄今未被注意到的某个特征的手段。当我们的目标是让这部电影出局时，关注这一特征可能就会产生消极的审美差异。不过，它也可以产生积极的审美差异——作为一个论据，说明为什么这部电影比其他参赛电影更好。

事实上，这就是评论家应该做的，不仅是在他们作为评委的时候，而且在他们写影评的时候也是如此。这就是优秀评论家的实际所为：不像美国标志性电影评论家宝琳·凯尔（1919—2001）那样，把评论当作一种艺术形式；不总结电影情节；不讲述他们那些与电影情节有着松散联系的童年记忆；不告诉我们他们喜欢什么，不喜欢什么。评论家的工作是把我们的注意力引到那些我们除非经提醒否则不会注意到的特征上。对其中一些特征的关注可以彻底改变我们的体验。

其中一些特征可能是结构性的，比如，小说第12页的主题是如何在第134页以及之后的第432页和第563页重新出现，这又如何给原本非结构的叙事提供了一种结构。另外一些特征可能关乎那些与其他艺术作品的联系——例如，一部音乐作品如何引用另一部音乐作品中的曲调。对其中一些特征的关注可能会让我们的体验更有价值。这就使得阅读评论文章的努力是值得的。

这里有一个现实生活中的例子：一小幅15世纪意大利油画，描绘的是"天使报喜"（见图4）。画家（多梅尼科·维内齐亚诺，约1410—1461）在轴对称上开了一点小玩笑：这座对称的建筑偏离了中心，它被推到画面中间偏左的位置。"动作"也偏离了中心，但它被推到了右边，而不是左边。注意这三个对称轴之间的相互影响（建筑物、这幅画本身以及圣母玛利亚和大天使之间的对称轴），并不是每个人都能立即发觉。但当它被指出来，你的注意力因此被吸引到它身上时，就会产生巨大的审美差异。

就纯粹的数量而言，从来没有像今天这么多的评论（文章），因为如今存在着成千上万个博客和网站。但这只是更明显地表明，评论正处于危机之中。正如英国文学评论家特里·伊格尔顿（1943—　）在三十多年前（远在博客出现之前）所痛陈的那样，"今天的评论缺乏一切实质性的社会功能。它要么是文学产业公共关系的一部分，要么完全是院校内部的事务"。自那以后，有一件事发生了变化，那就是出现了一些名流评论家，他们对电影、音乐和电视节目发表评论（通常是当着现场观众的面），除此之外，他们什么都没做。但是，如果评论家只做他们该做的事，即引导读者关注那些可以产生审美差异的特征，那么评论的社会功能就可以得到恢复。

法国小说家安德烈·马尔罗（1901—1976）曾说过，写艺术评论的主要目的不是让读者理解艺术，而是说服她爱上艺术。对艺术发表高谈阔论当然容易得多，但评论家只有在帮助读者以一种能说服读者爱上作品的方式去关注作品时，才算是在做她自己的本职工作。

66

图 4　多梅尼科·维内齐亚诺的《天使报喜》(15 世纪)，藏于剑桥菲茨威廉博物馆

67

现实生活中的审美一致

奇怪的是，我在担任电影节评委期间学到的另一个重要经验不是关于审美分歧，而是关于审美一致。我发现自己一次又一次地认同一些评论家的观点，尽管他们来自完全不同的大陆，而且常常比我大五十岁左右。这让我感到很好奇，该怎么解释生活在美国的二十多岁的匈牙利人和生活在中国香港的七十多岁的阿根廷人在审美评价上的趋同。

而且我越来越多地注意到，这些电影评论家和我是看着非常类似的电影长大的。在电影节提供的电影中，我们喜欢同样的电影，因为我们在青少年时期看的电影已经让我们喜欢上它们了。这在当时是一种直觉，但事实证明，有一些强有力的心理学研究结果支持这种直觉。

正如我们前文所示的那样，纯粹接触效应是一种众所周知的现象，即之前重复接触某种刺激会更有可能对该刺激做出正面评价，而且这种效应也存在于审美领域。但在两种不同的纯粹接触研究结果之间要做一个重要的区分。我在第四章提到的实验（康奈尔大学教授在课堂上展示看似随机呈现的印象派绘画的幻灯片），是关于让你接触一幅**特定的画**会如何让你更喜欢**那幅画**。但其他纯粹接触的研究结果是关于某类**特定的输入**会如何让你更喜欢**那类输入**。所以，看很多印象派的画会让你 68 喜欢上另一幅你从未见过的印象派画作。也就是说，你以前看过的艺术作品，会对你以后喜欢什么样的艺术作品产生深远的影响。

如果你在成长时期看过20世纪60年代法国和意大利的黑

白形式主义电影，那么你会喜欢在大致风格上类似于这些电影的电影（在摄影构图或叙事方面），而且无论你是在布达佩斯长大还是在布宜诺斯艾利斯长大，都确实如此。

纯粹接触效应在音乐方面可能更加突出：你在性格形成时期听的音乐类型（尤其是幼年时期和青少年时期的接触）会对你成年后所喜欢的音乐产生巨大影响。音乐品位会改变——而且通常会有很大的改变。但这并不意味着你原先的最爱会被重写覆盖。他们总是会对你喜欢什么样的音乐产生影响。

我在第四章中写了纯粹接触效应的一些令人担忧的方面，即我们的审美偏好变化是多么不明显。但纯粹接触效应也不全是坏事。认识到我们的审美偏好是如何根植于我们特定的文化和知觉背景，可以帮助我们放下我们的审美傲慢，并促使我们走向审美谦逊。

审美谦逊

如果你从八岁就开始听激流金属音乐，你的审美偏好会与那些只听传统印尼甘美兰音乐长大的人截然不同。到目前为止都没有什么让人惊讶的。你会对那些甘美兰乐迷听不到的细微差别很敏感。你能够关注激流金属乐中鲜有人会注意到的特征。

如果我想搞清楚该去听"超级杀手合唱团"的哪张专辑，我可能会相信你，而不是我的甘美兰鉴赏家朋友，因为你会是更可靠的信息来源。但这事并不是就此完结了。纯粹接触激流金属乐会让你对某些音乐形式和节奏有审美偏好，这可能会影响你对其他音乐作品的参与。

69

假设我让你和我爱听甘美兰音乐的朋友听一些20世纪早期的维也纳无调性音乐或者一些非常不和谐的纽约自由爵士乐，你会喜欢上其中一些作品，也会厌恶另外一些作品。但让你喜欢这首音乐而不是那首的部分原因是你曾接触过激流金属乐。（我希望大家明白，我在这里并不是要排斥激流金属乐——如果一个受过非调性训练的人第一次听激流金属乐，也会发生同样的情况。）但是我那位受过甘美兰音乐训练的朋友由于接触过甘美兰音乐，所以会喜欢不同的曲子。

你可能会说这里存在审美上的分歧。但分歧真的存在吗？这个例子告诉我们，我们是根据过去接触的特定艺术品（和其他刺激物）的特定视角来进行审美评价的。这并不意味着我们过去的接触完全决定了我们的审美评价。但它是这些审美评价的基础，且总是会出现在这些评价中。从这个意义上说，所有的审美评价都与评价者的文化和知觉背景紧密相连或挂钩。你对无调性音乐作品的评价与你的激流金属乐文化背景有关。我的朋友对同一件音乐作品的评价与她的甘美兰音乐背景有关。

要问谁对谁错是没有意义的。如果审美评价与评价者的文化背景有关，那么这里就没有真正的审美分歧，因为你的评价是根据激流金属乐文化背景，而我的甘美兰音乐朋友的评价是根据另一种非常不同的文化背景。

这并不意味着没有审美评价的事实；也不意味着一说到美学，怎么都行。这只表明审美评价是与评价者的文化背景有关。如果两个评价者有相同的文化背景而且他们意见不同，这的确是一个真正的审美分歧——他们中的一个人可能是对的，另一个可能是错的。

我举这个激流金属乐/无调性音乐的例子有点极端。没有人只听一种音乐。即使你是一个狂热的激流金属乐迷，你也无法完全过滤掉所有其他的音乐（就像在商场播放的贾斯汀·比伯的音乐）。但这并不能改变这一论据的效力，即你的审美评价受你的文化背景影响。由此可见，在进行审美评价时，你应该意识到自己的文化背景。你的审美评价并不是什么普遍的标准。这是一件非常独特的个人事项，深深根植于你非常偶然的文化背景中。因此，我们应该以相当谦虚的态度对待所有的审美

71　事项。

美
学

第六章

美学与生活

美学讨论各种特殊时刻。但这些时刻是我们枯燥日常生活中的孤岛吗？我不这么认为。如果幸运的话，你可以在早餐前获得三次以上的审美体验。

但是，艺术以及我们与所有美好事物的接触，也可能会以一种更加平淡的方式影响着我们的生活。你穿得像你最喜欢的电影中的某个角色（可能你都没有意识到），你使用着你从情景喜剧中学到的短语。正如前卫摄影师贝伦妮斯·阿博特（1898—1991）所说的那样，欣赏摄影作品有助于人们看清事物。美学与生活在各个层面上都是相互交织在一起的。

把生活看作一件艺术品？

审美对我们生活的重要性并不意味着我们必须求助于廉价的励志自助口号。有一种极受欢迎且极具影响力的观点是，我们应该把我们的生活变成（或者把我们的生活看作）一件艺术品。我想讲清楚我所说的与这种观点有何不同。

从约翰·沃尔夫冈·冯·歌德（1749—1832）和弗里德里希·尼采（1844—1900）到马塞尔·杜尚（1887—1968），在"西方"现代性中的每一个重要人物都认可这种比喻的某些版本。以至于奥地利小说家、《没有个性的人》的作者罗伯特·穆齐尔（1880—1942）把这条自助建议夸大到了极限，并以此寻开心：

> 这是一种什么样的生活，人们必须不断打下被称作"假期"的窟窿？我们应该在一幅画上打孔吗，因为它对我们的审美要求太高了？

如果你眯起眼睛看，你会发现这种把生活看作一件艺术品的观点在19世纪是有道理的，当时的艺术作品都是建构良好且连贯的整体。我能看到有人努力把他们的生活变成简·奥斯汀（1775—1817）的小说——它按照顺序有开头，有中间部分，有结尾；而且用一个漂亮连贯的、常常感人至深的情节发展把这些部分串起来。但是，要把你的生活变成玛格丽特·杜拉斯（1914—1996）的小说（实际上什么也没有发生）或者罗贝托·波拉尼奥（1953—2003）的小说（只会发生可怕的事情），将会是一件非常不确定的事情。

更普遍的问题是，艺术变得太像生活了。事实上，在过去的半个世纪左右（至少从激浪派艺术和大众艺术开始），艺术运动的大口号就是艺术不应该脱离生活。所以，如果艺术变得像生活，那么把你的生活变成一件艺术品要么毫无意义，要么纯粹是不合时宜。甚至有一种视觉艺术的亚流派，艺术家在他们的画

美学

布上挖出真实的洞,这就使得引述穆齐尔的话更加滑稽可笑。

但也许我不够宽容。也许这里的主题思想并不是应把我们的生活变成一件艺术品,而是我们对待生活的态度应该像对待一件艺术品一样。

采用这种方法的也不乏令人羡慕的偶像大咖。阿尔贝·加
缪（1913—1960）在他那部被大多数人遗忘的小说《快乐的死》（1938）中写道:“就像所有的艺术品一样,生活也要求我们去思考它。”这句话很好,但提到艺术品其实就像障眼法一样在转移他人的注意力。很多事情都需要我们去思考,诸如哲学书籍、白宫新闻,以及灰姑娘的鞋子如果非常合脚为什么会掉下来这一谜题。

所以在这方面把生活比作艺术品并不是特别有用。尽管有些艺术品确实需要思考,但什么样的明确思想才适合作为对《勃兰登堡协奏曲》（1721）或蒙德里安画作的回应呢?加缪的妙语警句并没有给“未经检验的生活不值得活”的旧咒语增添任何新意。

很多东西都可以成为艺术,而且与艺术品有很多关联方式,但没有一种方式天生就比另一种好。因此,敦促我们把我们的生活变成一件艺术品,或者把生活当成一件艺术品来对待,既没有帮助,也没有特别的意义。

做自己生活的旁观者?

还有一种将美学与我们的生活联系起来的流行方式,我希望与之保持安全距离。在某种程度上,这是“把你的生活当作一件艺术品”的观点的一个版本,不过这是一个非常具体的版本。

其要旨是，对待生活和艺术品的正确态度是超然的旁观者。正如王尔德所说，我们应该成为自己生活的旁观者。

这种理念在19世纪和20世纪的大部分时间里都很有影响力。过去几百年里在"西方"创作的许多艺术作品，显然都在追求这种效果。我在本书中引用过的许多文学大师（从佩索阿到普鲁斯特）都非常赞同这种审美参与的观点。就连苏珊·桑塔格，尽管在其他方面对全面的艺术主张有着非常敏锐的洞察力，但也紧跟这一潮流，她说："所有伟大的艺术都会引起沉思，一种动态的沉思。"

认真考虑注意力在审美体验中的作用，其中一个好处就是：我们可以解释这种超然的沉思体验为何一直是一个重要隐喻，而且也可以解释它如何没有成为所有审美参与的一个必要特征。桑塔格、普鲁斯特或佩索阿所说的那种参与，可以被描述为在艺术品的各个特征之间自由移动的开放式注意力。

正如我们所看到的那样，这种注意力运用方式反映了一种特定历史和地理条件下的审美体验形式，它与那种被称为冥想的体验相当吻合。不过，这仍然只是一种审美体验，不管它在20世纪上半叶的欧洲有多大的影响力。审美体验并不一定是超然的，未必是沉思的，而且也未必涉及开放式注意力。

就20世纪30年代的许多政治事件来看，许多赞同"成为自己生活的旁观者"这一观点的虔诚信徒都变得对这个概念非常怀疑。法国小说家安德烈·纪德（1869—1951）在希特勒执政一年后的1934年于日记中写道："今天，无论是谁，只要还在沉思，要么表现出的是一种毫无人性的生活信条，要么是一种骇人的盲目。"

美
学

更概括地说，强调沉思似乎与艺术中不可否认的政治因素相违背。沉思常被视为与政治无关；但在动荡年代，选择沉思静观而不是政治活动，常常遭受怀疑。

不管我们如何看待美学，我们都不应该不假思索地把政治学从美学领域移除，也不应该把美学从政治学领域移除。对沉思的强调很容易导致政治学和美学之间的某种尖锐对立，但是任何这样的对立从历史学和心理学角度来看都是不准确的。

与此相反，审美行为一直是而且仍然是政治思想的重要载体。事实上，这是美学社会意义的一个重要方面。我年轻时最难忘的审美体验，是1988年反对苏联占领匈牙利的一次示威活动，当时我们完全出乎意料地可以在一大群人中反复自由地高呼"俄国人滚回家"，而不必担心警察的镇压。我非常喜欢司汤达对这种关系的诠释（它也强调了注意力的概念）："在文学作品中，政治就像音乐会中的一声枪响。虽然有点俗气，但确实能让每个人立刻关注起来。"

那要是对自己生活的沉思会怎么样？美好的生活就是与我们的生活保持一种沉思的关系，这一观点与强调沉思性审美体验密切相关。很容易看出，这如何成为当前最新的一些励志自助学派——如斯多葛派/佛教复兴或正念——会极力利用的一句话。我们看到，当代艺术已经抛弃了沉思。而且，沉思在我们艺术世界里的作用越来越小，正因为如此，正念产业才很容易占领这个利基市场。

生活和美学之间的关系远比冥想的陈词滥调更重要，更有价值。审美体验可以帮助我们避开厌倦。它们可以教会我们许多看世界的新方法。

如何不让人厌倦？

我谈到了做电影节评委教会我的经验。但担任评委也有令人沮丧的一面。你必须花很多时间与其他评委在一起，他们中的许多人已经在这一行做了几十年。

也许我是不幸的，但我不得不花很多时间和那些让人非常厌倦的评委在一起。他们（经常大声地）说他们是多么热爱电影，但我几乎没有看到这方面的迹象。他们对我们一起看的每一部电影都加以抱怨，即使是那些他们并不完全讨厌的电影，他们也只是从评奖意见或影评该怎么说的角度来欣赏。

我放弃了评委工作，决定过一种不那么光鲜的学术生活，是因为我不想成为他们那样的人。我不想变得让人厌烦。我不想忘记如何真正地受到一部电影或其他艺术作品的打动、感动和振奋。

但是，这些人做错了什么？他们是如何变得如此令人厌烦的？举个例子吧：就拿罗尼（这可能是也可能不是他的真名）来说。罗尼是个英国人——地道的英国人。他为英国一家顶级报纸撰稿，但他也在英国几乎所有的优质纸质媒体那里做兼职。他不年轻了。他青年时代生活在巴黎，在20世纪60年代的文学和电影界中与让娜·莫罗和让-吕克·戈达尔那类人过从甚密。这是他作为电影评论家的全部身份的背景基础：在电影史上这个充满活力和激动人心的时期，他与演员们在如今被视为经典的电影片场中喝得酩酊大醉。

尽管我们有年龄差距，我和罗尼还是成了非常好的朋友，部分原因是我们在艺术和电影方面的品味惊人地一致。不过，罗

美
学

尼把每一部当代电影都和他钟爱的经典电影作比较；如果你花了半辈子的时间在电影节上，这可不是什么特别有益的态度，因为你的工作就是看当代电影。而罗尼的态度在电影评论家中并不罕见：我在这些圈子里看到了很多文化悲观主义和对过去的颂扬。如果这些电影评论家能从观看老电影而非新电影中得到乐趣，那么他们可能就在电影节上浪费了时间。不过，或许他们一点也不感到厌倦。他们只是看错了电影。或许我一开始就是这么想的。

在芝加哥国际电影节的一个晚上，在经历了特别艰难的评委会评审决定并喝了大量的意大利苦杏仁酒之后，罗尼承认，他再也无法从观看他原来最喜欢的电影中获得任何乐趣。他说，他有时能理解这些电影与其他电影的一些有趣联系，或者注意到一些细微的差别，然后他可以在一些评论或文章中写出来。但他已经没有任何感觉了。可以理解，罗尼对此很烦恼。我也是。

从那时起，我就意识到这是一个在专业艺术评论家甚至艺术史学家中相当普遍的现象。恩斯特·贡布里希（1909—2001）可能是20世纪最知名的艺术史学家，也面临着同样的困境。他可以对他看过的几乎任何一幅画进行细致入微的艺术和历史分析，但整个经历却让他完全麻木。

事实上，我已经开始惊恐地注意到我自己身上的这种迹象。我越来越不喜欢看电影了，尤其是当我知道我必须写一篇影评的时候。而且我不得不承认，罗尼在看完一部电影后，能坐下来在十分钟内写出一流的、复杂而知识渊博的两页影评，这一点非常了不起。因此，我在想，也许成为一名真正专业的电影评论家要付出的代价，是否就是我们必须停止欣赏电影？这种可能性把我吓坏了。也许这种艺术享受的事只适合业余爱好者？真正的专业人士不会在这上面浪费时间？

　　　我认为自己没有给这些问题一个很好的答案。但我担任电影评论家的这段时间，教会我看清罗尼和他的同事们（而且至少在一段时间内，甚至包括自己）所做的是什么：当他们坐在电影院里时，他们对要看的内容有着非常明确和固定的期待。

甜蜜的和不那么甜蜜的期待

　　期待是一件好事。如果我们对周围的事物没有期待，我们能做之事就寥寥无几。期待在我们与艺术的接触中也起着至关重要的作用：当我们听一首歌时，即使是第一次听到，我们也会对它将如何继续展开有一些期待。当它是我们熟悉的乐段时，这种期待就可能非常强烈（而且很容易通过实验进行研究）。在贝多芬的《第五交响曲》（1808）的开头听到"嗒—嗒—嗒"的时候，我们会强烈地期待"嗒—嗒—嗒—嗒啊姆"的结尾。

　　有很多科学研究是关于期待如何影响我们对音乐、痛苦以及一切事物的体验。我们的许多期待都非常不确定：当我们在听一段我们从未听过的音乐时，我们仍然会对一个乐段如何继续产生一些期待，但我们不知道具体会发生什么。我们可以排除小提琴滑音会伴随着闹钟的"哔哔"声继续演奏（除非这是一个非常前卫的作品），但我们不能很确定地预测它会如何继续演奏。我们的期待易受影响且会动态变化：它们随着我们对这首曲子的聆听而变化。

　　我怀疑那些已感到厌倦的评论家的期待不是那么易受影响，不怎么有动态性。罗尼准确地知道他在熄灯后的期待是什么。毫无疑问，有时这部电影会让他感到意外；但即便如此，也会以一种意料之中的方式让他感到意外："啊哈，对了，导演选择了一种让人想起希区柯克而不是悲观色彩影片的叙事转折！"这部电影能够做到的各种可能空间在一开始就已经被他在脑海中勾勒出来了。唯一不确定的是，电影会以哪一种已得到非常确切的界定与充分理解的规则来结尾。

当然，你对电影了解得越多，你就会有更多的比较模式，在电影中做任何以前没有做过的事情都是非常困难的。如果你对整个电影史了如指掌，就很难忽视这些潜在的共同点、差异和类似。但这可能会让你的体验变成纯粹的分类工作：故事情节就像《夺宝奇兵》（1981），摄影构图就像《阿凡达》（2008），表演就像《大人物拿破仑》（2004）。这样看电影就没有多少乐趣可言。

这里缺少的是某种程度的谦虚开明，以及让自己真正感到惊讶的意愿。不仅要惊讶于这部电影最后属于哪一种得到精心划分的电影史分类，也要惊讶于这部电影对你的影响。

这位厌倦的电影评论家注意力非常集中。罗尼会重点关注他认为与他的评论相关的几个界定清晰的特征，而且他会忽略其他的一切。通常情况下，这是正确的，因为剩下的事情很可能都可以预测到。但有时会出现无法预测的情况，罗尼就会错过他注意力焦点之外的任何事情。

但是，如果我们不是带着界定清晰的期待（或者我应该说先入之见？）去看一部电影，那么我们就不会立即忽略那些我们认为有价值的特征范围之外的所有东西。每件事都可能具有价值，即使是那些专业评论家认为是浪费时间的东西。

安德烈·布勒东（1896—1966），诗人、艺术家，20世纪20年代和30年代巴黎超现实主义运动的元老，不太喜欢电影。他发现它太容易预测，太真实，不太符合他的超现实主义标准。但他找到了一种欣赏电影的方法，那就是把张开的左手放在眼前，这样他就看不到整个屏幕，只能看到其中的一部分。他声称以这种方式获得了很棒的体验。这不是罗尼会做的事，坦白地说，这也不是我向任何初露头角的电影评论家推荐要做的事，但这显然比罗尼的体验更有乐趣。

就在布勒东通过遮住屏幕的一半，安德烈·布勒东成功摆脱了他对将要发生的事情的先入之见，他可以对屏幕上的东西有一种真正开放式的体验。这又是一个极端的例子，显然并不适用于所有人。（想象一下观众们捂着眼睛的场面，这可不是每个导演的梦想。）但是，这就是安德烈·布勒东对抗倦怠倾向的方式。他所做的就是强迫自己的注意力不去寻找那些人们都关注的、老一套的东西。他强迫自己的注意力开放，不受期待约束。肯定有办法不遮住眼睛就能做到这一点。

以全新视角看待

就在布勒东通过手指缝看电影的同一时期，意大利画家乔治·德·基里科（1888—1978）也在画着令人难以忘怀但又有些令人不安的美丽画作，画中有空旷的广场、拱门、古代雕塑和远处的火车。他有一种特殊的才能，能把日常生活的场景变成现实世界之外的东西。他对此也做了很多说明：

一个晴朗的秋日下午，我坐在佛罗伦萨圣十字广场中央的长椅上。这当然不是我第一次看这个广场了。[……]

美
学

整个世界，一直到建筑物的大理石和喷泉，在我看来都像是在逐渐康复之中。广场中央耸立着一尊但丁的雕像，他披着一件长斗篷，手捧着他的作品，戴着桂冠的头若有所思地向下低着。这座雕像是用白色大理石塑成，但时间把它浇铸成了浅灰色，非常悦目。秋天的阳光温暖却又冷漠，照亮了雕像和教堂的正面。于是我有了一种奇怪的感觉，觉得自己是第一次看到这些东西。

我发现这段引用最准确的地方是最后一句。当我们在一件艺术品或风景前产生强烈的体验时，我们经常就像第一次看到它一样去观看它。事实上，描述某些形式的审美体验特征的一个好方法，就是让人感觉这是我们第一次经历这种体验。即使我们以前见过很多次，但当它真正触动我们的时候，感觉就像第一次看见一样。我们以前从未**真正**见过它。但现在我们看见了。

"第一次看到它"这句台词听起来可能像一句陈词滥调，但我认为不止如此。当你第一次看到某样东西时，你没有用既定的常规方法去看待它，即挑出那些你认为有价值的特征，而忽略其他特征。你会移动你的注意力，因为它的任何特征都可能是有价值的。因此，当你第一次看到某样东西时，你的注意力往往是开放式的——你不清楚该关注什么。

如果你突然需要扑灭朋友公寓里的火，而你第一次看到一个物体（甚至是一件艺术品），你可能不会将注意力放在四处寻找有价值的特征上。你会留意寻找的只有一件事：它如何能帮助你灭火。但是，如果你不急于去做某件特定的事情，而且你对一件你从未见过的东西感兴趣（而这就是在博物馆通常发生的事情），你的注意力往往是开放式的。第一次看到某样东西的感觉表明你的注意力是开放的。

当产生第一次看到某样东西的感觉时，你已经抛弃了任何既定、常规的看待它的方式。这就是我感兴趣的比较：常规的、习惯性的看待事物的方式和"好像是第一次"看待事物的方式。这就是德·基里科所讨论的内容：他那常规且习惯性的与世界相连的方式突然停止了，于是他以全新视角来看待这个世界。

当然，常规和习惯性没有什么不对。在开车上班的路上，在交通堵塞的情况下行车，若能有一种常规且习惯性的感知方式就太好了：在这种情况下，你不会想去重新审视事物。而且，重新审视的维持时间很难超过几分钟。你不可能每时每刻都处于这种审美的出神状态。

还记得你十几岁时反复听的那首歌吗？每次都让你印象深刻。直到你不再被它震撼。就好像你把它消耗殆尽；你对它太习以为常了。每当这种事发生在我身上，我都有一种真正的失落感。

值得高兴的是，至少有时候这种体验还能重现。你停止聆听这首歌一段时间，几个月（或几年）后，当你再次听到它时，它可能会比以往任何时候都更让你震撼。而且，你会觉得好像是第一次聆听一样。那些习惯和常规都消失了。

这是德·基里科和他的巴黎朋友们在一百年前提出的重要观点：艺术可以帮助我们克服日常感知中平淡无奇的习惯和常规。习惯会消磨你。即使是最美丽的事物，你看得越多，也会变得越来越逊色。但是艺术可以帮助你摆脱你的习惯，并让你以一种从未有过的方式来看待某件事。

这种"以全新视角看待"的感觉显然不能捕捉到我们在审美体验中所在意的一切。正如我们所看到的那样，并不是所有的审美体验都以这种开放式的注意力为特征——当你看到那些事物时，就像你第一次看到它们一样。毫无疑问，我们会珍惜将一首歌听几百遍、反复看同样的电影一直到记住所有台词之类的体验。当我们这样做的时候，我们确实喜欢那种熟悉的感觉。马塞尔·杜尚甚至把艺术称作"一种让人上瘾的药物"。审美体验有不同的特色。但有些审美体验与我们看待事物是否像第一次看到它那样有很大关系。

挥之不去的影响

这里还有审美影响我们生活的另一种方式。审美体验会产生一种挥之不去的影响。这是欣赏艺术的过程中奇怪而又未得到充分探讨的一个方面：它挥之不去，久久不散。当你在博物馆里待了一整天，然后步行回家时，单调乏味的公交车站在你看来可能就像博物馆里的一幅画。当你听完一场精彩的音乐会或看完一场电影后，丑陋、灰暗、肮脏的街景看起来反而很美。

马塞尔·普鲁斯特描述了同样的现象。在欣赏了他最喜欢的画家的作品后（他用虚构的名字埃尔斯特来指代他），他开始注意到他以前从未注意过的平淡无奇的餐厅特征。他看到他以前看到过很多很多次的场景变得截然不同了。突然，他开始关注：

> 餐刀依然交叉地堆叠成残缺的姿势；废弃的餐巾纸鼓鼓地放在那里，阳光照在上面像打了块黄色天鹅绒补丁；半

空的玻璃杯弧形曲面更显高贵之气，而且，在像冰冻的阳光那样透彻的透明水晶玻璃中间，有一滴红酒残渣，颜色暗淡却因反射光而闪闪发亮；固体物品的位移，随着光影的流动而变化着；盘中被吃掉一半的李子不断改变颜色，从绿色到蓝色，再从蓝色到金黄色；那些椅子，像一群老太太，每天两次，围绕铺着白色桌布的桌子就座，就像庆祝味觉仪式的圣餐台那样，凹陷的牡蛎壳就像一个小的石质圣水池，里面聚集着几滴净水……

正如他所说的那样，"我试图在我以前从未想象过它会存在的地方、在最普通的事物中、在'静物'的深度中找到美"。

强调注意力在审美参与中的重要性的一个好处是，它可以解释这个令人困惑的现象。艺术改变了你的关注方式。这种专注的状态不会就这样停止而是一直存在。

审美体验可以让我们抛弃我们对所见事物先入之见的理解方式。当我们体验完这件艺术品，我们的注意力自由状态需要一段时间才能改回来。我们以开放式注意力不断地靠近我们所看到的任何事物，而这可能会导致电影院前肮脏的人行道被视为一件艺术品。

美国抽象派画家阿德·莱因哈特（1913—1967）这样说道："留意观看并不像它看起来那么简单。艺术教会人们如何留意观看。"这是我们从欣赏艺术中获得的一个重大好处：它可以让你恢复简单的视觉快乐——不管你看到的是什么。它**可以让你**就像第一次看到它们那样去看待事物。

第七章

全球性美学

回想一下你上次参观大型艺术博物馆的情景。你能回忆起博物馆里"必看"的艺术品中有多少是在欧洲或美国创作的吗?可能绝大多数都是吧。但是世界各地都会创作艺术作品,而不仅仅是在欧洲和美国。这些艺术品在大多数艺术博物馆却都难以找到。哪怕它们确实在馆里,也往往会被藏在某个偏远的侧翼展厅里。

抽象表现主义画家威廉·德·库宁(1904—1997)将艺术史的当代主流观点比作铁轨:"艺术史上有一条火车轨道可以追溯到美索不达米亚,但它跳过了整个东方、玛雅和美洲印第安人。杜尚在这条轨道上面;塞尚在上面;毕加索和立体派画家在上面;贾科梅蒂、蒙德里安以及许多其他艺术家——全部文明都在上面。"

幸运的是,如今很少有艺术史学家认同这种单一轨道的艺术史观。但这种对艺术的思考方式仍然主导着日常的艺术概念,也主导着大多数博物馆的管理工作。如果我们想要停止赋予欧洲艺术于其他艺术之上的特权地位,我们不仅需要改变"西方"艺术和"非西方"艺术之间的不平衡,还需要改变"西方"美学和"非西方"美学之间的不平衡。我们需要一种全球性美学。

视域的地理性

你成长的文化环境是如何决定你的审美体验(你对艺术品、风景等的体验)的呢?这是全球性美学的起始问题。而答案也很简单:我们不能想当然地认为,所有地方、所有历史时期的工艺品都按照此时此地的感知方式去感知。(从现在开始,我将使用"工艺品"进行讨论,因为我不想讨论在哪些文化中什么可以算作艺术,而什么不能算作艺术品的问题。)

这一主张与传统的美学观点相悖——根据传统美学的观点,美学作为一门学科是讨论共性的:它研究的是独立于我们的文化背景,与艺术品和其他审美对象进行接触的方式。事实上,艺术史学家经常指责美学家的这种文化普遍性。这种美学普世主义在美学研究中得到了更多的强调,这些研究最近受很时髦的神经科学污染,通常旨在以一种不依赖于受试文化背景的方式,找到各种审美形式的神经关联。

事实上,这正好相反。如果我们认真对待大脑的各种实验科学,它们教会我们的实际上就是彻底抛弃文化普遍性。其中的原因是,有大量的文献充分证明了自上向下对感知的影响。成千上万的心理学和神经科学研究表明,我们所知道和相信的东西甚至会影响到视觉和听觉处理的最初阶段。考虑到我们对不同事物的认识和信仰取决于我们成长的文化和时期,我们的感知也会根据我们成长的文化和时期不同而有所不同。

这里的问题是,这些自上而下对感知的影响是如何发挥作用的，又是什么样的过程促使它们发挥作用。我将讨论两种这样的调解机制，即注意力和心理意象。注意力和心理意象都严重依赖于我们更高阶的心理状态，如信念和知识。而且注意力和心理意象都会影响我们的感知和审美参与。

换言之，注意力和心理意象存在跨文化差异。考虑到注意力和心理意象在我们审美参与中的重要性，这就注定我们的审美参与也会存在跨文化差异。既然我们已经知道大脑是如何运作的，那么文化普遍性就无法成立了。我们不能假设我们的审美参与和当地工艺品生产者和用户意图要达到的以及已实施的审美参与是相同的。

我们关注什么以及如何关注，在很大程度上取决于我们的信念、知识和感知能力背景，而这些都有文化特定性。所以我们的注意力模式也具有文化特定性。不过，考虑到我们对工艺品的体验在很大程度上取决于我们所关注的东西，这意味着我们对工艺品的体验存在着显著的跨文化差异。

这里有一个例子：请看图5中所示的所罗门群岛的护胸甲。你可能会看到一个由相交线组成的抽象图案。现在我要告诉你们，这个护胸甲下端的倒V形很可能是军舰鸟的尾巴，而其上面的形状是它的翅膀。这只军舰鸟表明这里有成群的鲣鱼，这种鱼是圣克鲁斯群岛居民的重要食物，而这只护胸甲就来自该群岛。人们认为再往上的形状表示海豚或鱼，甚至可能是军舰鸟所发出的表示有鲣鱼的信号。

在阅读前一段内容之前和之后，你可能会注意到这个护胸甲的不同特点。你会把更多的注意力放在你之前忽略的部分上（例如，可能代表海豚背鳍的小突起）。因此，你的体验是截然不

图5 护胸甲,产于19世纪晚期的所罗门群岛(大洋洲),收藏于大都会艺术博物馆

同的。(特定文化上的)注意力变化会导致你对工艺品的体验发生变化。

　　不同文化间的差异不仅在于我们关注的内容,还在于我们关注的方式。在东亚长大的人对简单的视觉展示的反应与欧洲人不同,例如在看一个水族箱时,欧洲人倾向于关注游动的鱼,而东亚人倾向于关注背景特征,比如气泡或海藻。总体来说,欧洲人在这些视觉任务中的注意力似乎更集中,而东亚人的注意力则更分散。同样,注意力的运用也存在着跨文化差异,这就导致了我们体验中的跨文化差异。

自上而下影响知觉体验的第二个调解机制是心理意象。我们的心理意象很大程度上取决于我们所知道的和所相信的以及我们之前所感知到的其他事物。当你想象一个苹果时,这个想象出来的苹果的外貌取决于你在生活中见过的苹果种类。心理意象在我们的艺术体验中起着一种重要的作用。(这是日本美学中一个反复出现的主题。)

例如,印度尼西亚艺术家乔佩·库斯维达纳托(1976—　)创作了需要借助心理意象才能完成(体验)的装置作品。在这里,观众的心理意象是体验的一个重要组成部分(见图6)。

不同文化背景的人会使用不同的心理意象来完成对这个艺术品的体验——大概大多数人(并非所有人)在观看这个装置时会产生马的心理意象;但是,举个例子,在那些将马与战争联系在一起的文化中,这种心理意象(特别是骑手的形象)将会截然不同,而且它会携带着非常不同的情感负荷。这意味着有着不同文化背景的人,对同样的艺术作品会产生非常不同的体验。

库斯维达纳托装置对我们的心理意象有着异常直接和明确的要求。不过,几乎所有的艺术品体验都涉及心理意象。这在几乎所有的非"西方"美学传统中尤为明显,美学体验被非常明确地认为是一种多模态体验——它与我们所有的感官模式对话,不仅仅是视觉,还包括听觉、嗅觉、味觉和触觉(这种通常十分极端的视觉中心主义美学似乎就是一个"西方"的东西)。

这在"拉莎"传统中得到了最明确的表达,正如前文所看到

图6 乔佩·库斯维达纳托的《第三王国的队伍》，创作于2012年（印度尼西亚）

的那样，"拉莎"的字面意思是品味体验的情感味道。这里的味道不仅仅是一个比喻。即使是那些仅由一种感官模式（比如，在音乐例子中的听觉）触发的"拉莎"体验，也都运用了我们所有其他感官模式（视觉、嗅觉、触觉、味觉）。换句话说，它们应该唤起多模态心理意象。

而"拉莎"并不是一个孤立的案例。日本美学中一个关键概念是"隐美"，即"幽玄"，对它的欣赏涉及类似于（隐蔽而不完整面貌的）心理意象的东西。11世纪的伊斯兰哲学家阿维森纳也特别强调了意象在我们对美的体验中的重要性。

91

我们的体验取决于我们的文化背景。艺术史学家喜欢谈论视觉的历史。海因里希·沃尔夫林（1864—1945），可能是有史以来最具影响力的艺术史学家，他有一句名言："视觉本身有其历史，揭示这些视觉层级必须被看作艺术史的首要任务。"虽然关于这一挑衅性的说法已有很多讨论，但有一点合理性，即以下主张在经验上是正确的：考虑到注意力和心理意象都有其历史，受它们影响的视觉也有其历史。

如果从这个意义上说视觉有其历史，那么它也有地理环境意义。而且感知通常也是如此。考虑到注意力和心理意象的运用取决于我们在什么样的文化中长大，受这些文化影响的知觉也取决于我们的文化背景。全球性美学是关于视域的地理性。

一种全球性表达手段

我们不能用我们自己对一个工艺品的体验来假设在不同的文化中如何体验这个工艺品。但我们又该如何了解它在不同文化中（特别是在这些文化没有后继者可以与我们交谈的情况下）是如何体验和使用的呢？

我们对一些工艺品生产中心了解很多，对其他生产中心却了解很少。这就在全球性美学思想中引入了一种显著的不对称性。我们有相当多关于15世纪的意大利绘画是如何制作以及人们如何看待它们的信息，但我们对15世纪的中美洲几乎一无所知。这种认知的不对称性是由一些巧合因素造成的，比如有些地方记录保存了下来，而有些地方则没有保存下来。但这不应该让我们认为，世界上我们了解更多的那些地方的工艺品在某种程度上就更好或者更值得研究。

但是，如果我们不能把我们"西方的"经验外推到其他文化中，如果我们对如何体验世界大部分地区的工艺品了解甚少，这就会导致一个令人怀疑的结论：我们确实没有办法知道其他文化是如何体验工艺品的，因为在不同的文化中，对工艺品的体验

92

存在根本性的差异。如果我们想要避免这种令人怀疑的结论，我们就需要找到一种方法，在对工艺品产地文化了解不多的情况下，至少可以理解它们的某些方面。

全球性美学必须要有一个可以讨论任何工艺品的概念框架，不管这个工艺品在哪里制作以及何时制作。这相当于确定每一件工艺品都必须具有的且与美学相关的特征。

每件工艺品都需要有一些不重要的特征，包括材料组成和大小。每件工艺品都由某种材料做成，而且每件的尺寸要么是这么大，要么是那么大。还有一些更琐碎的特征，比如说这件工艺品描绘的是不是一个苹果。要么是，要么不是，没有其他选择。这些例子所存在的问题是：尽管在某些文化中，尺寸和材料构成可能与审美有关，但在其他许多文化中，它们则没有关联性。我们需要找到一些更具美学关联性的特征空间。

我想用图画作为案例研究。对图画的体验通常是一种审美体验，而且不仅是我们的"西方"文化如此认为。图画未必就是艺术作品，例如，关于如何在水上降落时逃离飞机的飞机安全图示，无论如何都不是艺术作品。很多东西都可视为图画：不仅是帆布上的油画、木头上的蛋彩画，还有皮肤上的文身、树皮上的划痕、手机上的自拍等。图画是各种各样的。

但是，每一幅图画都有图形组织：每一幅图画都以非随机的方式组织图形元素。图形组织在所有文化中都具有美学意义。"约鲁巴"美学（尼日利亚西南部人民的美学传统）的一个重要概念是"伊法拉洪"，它通常被翻译为"能见度"，即要求人的所有部位都成形清晰、明显可见。虽然这一概念最初被应用于雕塑，但它也成为应该被摄影师作为目标追求的最重要的优点（比如,这会意味着模特的双眼都应该是清晰可见的)。

在早期最翔实的中国绘画美学著作中,6世纪的中国画家和评论家谢赫概述了绘画的六大法则。其中第五个法则就是将图案要素根据空间和深度放置、排列在画的表面上。(这成为此后中国绘画论述的一个最重要主题。)《毗湿奴法上往世书》的第三部《坎达》,是一本极其详尽、百科全书式的印度教绘画文本,大约写于同一时期,也提到了很多图形组织——谁应该在谁的后面、旁边或前面。图形组织也一直是日本美学的一个重要话题。

所有这些作品所要问的问题是,图画是如何被组织起来的。在非常抽象的层面上,有两种不同而独特的图形组织模式,我称之为"表层组织"和"场景组织"。每一张图画,无论制作于何时何地,都处在表层组织和场景组织之间。

表层组织模式的目的,是吸引人们注意所描绘物体的二维轮廓形状,看它是如何放置在二维框架内的。相比之下,场景组织模式的目的是让人们注意到所描绘的三维物体是如何放置在所描绘的空间之内的。这两者之间存在着一种平衡,大多数图画都试图把它们结合起来使用。但是,当两种组织原则发生冲突时,其中一个原则——要么是场景原则,要么是表层原则——往往会胜出。

图形组织具有美学意义,因而所有的图画制作者需要选择如何组织他们的图画。而且,重要的是,这不是一个以"西方"为中心的区分,这是任何文化背景下的图画设计问题。因此,场景组织和表层组织之间的幅度范围可以作为一种非常笼统(但并非以"西方"为中心)的概念框架的一个起始点,用于描述任何图画——无论它们产自何处。

场景组织和表层组织之间的区别有点抽象。因此,通过更简单、更易发现的特性来证实这种区分会很有帮助。我将集中讨论两个这样的特征：遮挡和空白表面。

在日常的感知中，我们有很多遮挡：我们看到一些物体在其他物体的后面或前面。这里的问题是，遮挡是否会出现在图画中。表层组织模式意味着图画制作者注意到是否存在遮挡：图画中的遮挡是所描绘物体的二维轮廓形状在二维平面上相互联系的特征。有些图画会刻意避免遮挡；而其他一些图画则扎堆使用遮挡。这两者都是表层组织模式很好的标志。我们可以把所有的图画放在一个极度缺乏遮挡和极度寻求遮挡之间的频谱之上。图7和图8就是分别接近频谱两个极点的示例。

图7 斯基泰壁挂，公元前5世纪，发现于阿尔泰地区（西伯利亚）的巴泽雷克

图8　羽川藤永，《朝鲜通信使来朝图》（约1748年）

来自某些文化的图画会聚集在这个遮挡频谱某些特定点的周围。例如，巴泽雷克的斯基泰壁挂倾向于不惜一切代价地避免遮挡。在羽川藤永的图画中，几乎所有的东西似乎都被刻意遮挡住了。这两种类型的图画都可以算作表层组织模式。

相比之下，其他一些文化中的图画（例如，平面印第安人雕刻或17世纪的荷兰静物画），并不特别因为遮挡的有无而烦恼，这是一个场景组织模式的标志：如果一幅图是按照它所描绘的三维场景进行组织的，那么不管是遮挡还是缺乏遮挡都不是特别重要。

每幅图画都具有的第二个特征是空白表面的有无。在日常感知中，我们视域中一些部分经常是空白，因为那里没有引起感知兴趣的元素——只有天空、地面和一堵毫无意义的墙。有些

96

图画刻意避免出现空白表面：它们试图在表面的每一平方英寸上都放置有趣的图画元素。另一些则故意想获得空白表面。图9和图10就是一些示例。

图9　亚历山大·阿波斯托尔2001年作品《普利多公寓》（摄于委内瑞拉，
摄影师用数字技术删除了许多诸如门窗这样的建筑细节）

图 10 卧佛寺壁画所绘曼谷学院, 19世纪(泰国)

同样，关注表面的某些部分是否空白是表层组织模式的一个重要标志。场景组织模式对于表面的某些部分是否仍未得到填充没有倾向性。与遮挡情况一样，具有表层组织模式的图画会围绕空白表面频谱的某些特定点聚集（不同文化背景的图画围绕聚集的点不同）。相比之下，带有场景组织模式的图画聚集点则散布在这个频谱的大部分区域。

我们得到了一个基于遮挡和空白表面两个特征的坐标系。我们还可以添加其他特征，比如框架或对称性。有些图画遵守甚至强调自己的画框，有些则故意假装画框不存在。由于框架在很大程度上是一个二维表面特征，关注它（不管是通过强调还是淡化它）是表层组织模式的标志。对称性是另一个表面特征：刻意去获得对称的作品或者刻意去获得不对称的作品，就是表层组织模式的一个标志。如果对称性不是一个大问题（或者框架不是一个大问题），那么这就是场景组织模式的标志。

这就产生了一个多维特征空间，在这里我们可以放置每一张图画，不管我们对图画创作的文化有多少了解。这显然不是我们对来自不同文化的图画的全部理解：图画另外还有很多文化特有的特性是这种形式分析无法提供的。不过，这对任何进一步的、更具文化特定性的探究来说，都是一个坚实可靠的起点。

这种文化中立的多维特征空间可以促进我们更进一步理解我们知之甚少的那些文化中的图画。例如，如果在某个特定文化中产生的所有图画都刻意避免遮挡，这就给了我们一个重要的基准点，以探索他们这样做的原因。这种形式分析不会给我们答案（或者可能会给我们非常不完整的答案），但它可以让我们提出的问题更有针对性。

这里就有一个例子。如果你对中世纪欧洲文化一无所知，并且你看到了很多像我们在第五章（见图4）中遇到的多梅尼科·维内齐亚诺那副小型画作一样的图像，那么你就不会知道这些图像中的两个人物是谁。其中一个是女人，另一个有翅膀。但是，如果你看过足够多这个女人加上有翅膀的人体图案的图像，你就会注意到这两个人物往往被放置在离彼此很远的地方。它们不仅没有相互遮挡，而且以一种不可能相互遮挡的方式被置于画布之上。你不知道这些就是"天使报喜"的画面——是生活在不同精神世界的人类和天使之间的会面，因此，他们事实上不能（或不应该）被描绘在同一个空间里。只有了解了至少是中世纪欧洲的宗教和文化，你才会知道这一点。不过，即使你没有任何关于中世纪欧洲文化的信息，只要注意到这两个人物之间奇怪的空间关系，你至少可以识别出这种文化特有的奇怪之处。为了理解为何这成了中世纪《天使报喜》的一个设计问题，你就需要了解当地（中世纪欧洲）的文化。但是你也可以在没有任何特定文化信息的情况下注意到这个设计问题。

全球性美学建立在文化特定信息与每一种工艺品都共有的、非常普遍的形式特征之间相互加强的基础之上。这两个看似相反的倾向可以而且应该互相帮助：我们越了解某种文化中的工艺品所具有的某些反复出现的形式特征（例如，是否可以避免遮挡），我们就能更好地探寻他们为何这么做的某种特定文化信息。

在博物馆里进一步迷失

我在本书的一开始就谈了一种我们所有人在面对艺术品

或者其他具有审美意义的物品时都有过的体验——我们有时会发现无论我们多么努力都很难成功获得审美体验。你曾在这幅作品前有过强烈而有益的审美体验，但现在这种体验却没有发生。

这里有一个你在博物馆里可能更感纳闷、更具体的问题：当我遇到来自不同文化的工艺品时，我应该探寻什么？以贝宁的一个西非雕塑为例（见图11）。很有可能这些雕塑不应该有审美参与（不管我们对审美的释义多宽泛）。当你走进一个满是16世纪贝宁雕塑的博物馆时，你会怎么做？你想要什么样的体验呢？

我猜测，你正试图把这些物品与你所知道的艺术品联系起来以理解它们的意义。就西非雕塑而言，对我们许多人来说，这很可能是欧洲现代主义雕塑的参考系（而这并非偶然，它深受西非木雕的影响）。我们可能会被一些来自贝宁的雕塑所吸引，因为它们让我们想起了康斯坦丁·布朗库西（1876—1957）的现代主义雕塑（见图12）。我们可以从中获得相当多的审美愉悦，或许还有审美体验。

我曾提出过一个社会学观点：我描述了我们实际上是如何倾向于以这种方式接触这类物体的。不过，还有一个更进一步的问题：如果我们以这种方式与工艺品打交道，会是错误的吗？这些物品显然不是为了让人们像对待一件布朗库西作品一样去加以体验的。

这里有一个类似的问题：当我们遇到来自不同时期的工艺品时，我们要寻找什么呢？经常去博物馆意味着你会遇到来自不同时期的文物。听音乐或阅读文学作品也是如此。我们在遇

101

　　同样，我的社会学观点是，我们试图以一种我们可以与之关联的方式来体验这些作品：用我们体验当前作品时所熟悉的方式。当我们在第五章中看到多梅尼科·维内齐亚诺的画作时，

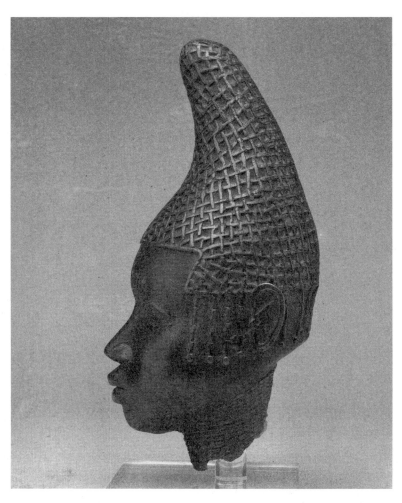

图11　《女王母亲的头》,16世纪（贝宁）

第七章　全球性美学

图 12　康斯坦丁·布朗库西,《麦雅斯特拉》(古根海姆博物馆)

　　我们试图用一种接触不同类型(比如20世纪)画作所形成的方式来看待它。问题依然存在:如果我们这样做了,是错误的吗?

　　鉴于我们审美体验的文化特殊性,在涉及艺术品的接触上甚至不会出现何谓正确何谓错误的问题。这些问题之所以不会出现,是因为在接触贝宁的雕塑和意大利早期的绘画时,无论将它们当作现代主义艺术来看待是否有错,我们都别无选择。我们所能做的就是从我们自己文化的角度来评价这些艺术品。

103

102

正如我们所看到的那样，审美体验受到一个人的文化背景自上而下的影响。贝宁雕刻家和雕塑的目标受众，在对审美参与自上而下的影响上，与我完全不同。这使得我们不太可能像这件工艺品最初的生产者和使用者那样对其进行接触。

但我们能不能至少试着弥合这个鸿沟呢？我们可以试一试。而且在某种意义上，我们也应该这样做。毋庸置疑，了解其他文化及其工艺品是非常有益的。不过，完全的文化渗透是几乎不可能的，这有一个系统的原因；而这就是一个我们现在非常熟知的心理现象：纯粹接触效应（整本书反复接触"纯粹接触效应"这个概念，应该会实实在在地让任何读者都对它产生深刻的印象）。由于纯粹接触效应，我们的价值判断取决于我们曾接触过的作品。我们根深蒂固的审美偏好（由我们在早期性格形成时期所遇到的情况所决定）是极其难以动摇的。

我们可以花几十年的时间**就地**探索一种不同的文化。事实上，许多世界艺术史学家都是这么做的。比如，如果他们研究印尼艺术，那么他们就搬到印尼住很多年，甚至几十年，把自己置于那种文化环境中，那个环境中的刺激可能与他们所习惯的刺激非常不同。而这至少可以部分逆转纯粹接触效应。但是生命是短暂的：比如说，即使你完全沉浸于印尼文化，你仍然会在一次玛雅艺术展中完全迷失。

再谈审美谦逊

英国艺术史学家和评论家迈克尔·巴克森德尔（1933—2008）区分了文化的参与者和观察者。正如他所说，"参与者以一种旁观者所不具备的即时性和自发性理解和认识（她的）文化。（她）可以在没有理性自我意识的文化标准和规范下行事"。

我的观点是，要完全成为一种不同文化的参与者是非常困难的，事实上，几乎是不可能的。默认情况是，尽管我们做出了所有努力，也只会永远保持观察者身份。仅仅因为我们读了几本关于大洋洲艺术的书，我们不会突然变成参与者。其原因主要还是以经验为依据的：自上而下对知觉的影响和纯粹接触效应。

对此该怎么做呢？仔细研究遥远的文化和艺术创作形式仍然是一个好主意，因为它可能非常有益。全球性美学至少应该向前走一段距离，去理解其他文化的人如何看待他们周围的世界。通过仔细研究遥远的文化，我们可以把它们拉近一点，而这就可以开启迄今未知的审美体验。但是任何人都不应被误导，以为这样做我们就能成为参与者，而不再仅仅是遥远的观察者。

于是，这就给了我们更多的理由去保持审美谦逊。我们应该始终意识到我们所占据的文化视角，并谦逊地对待我们的审美评价：把它看作从一个非常具体的文化视角做出的评价。我们很容易在美学上感到骄傲自大，或许正是因为它对我们个人来说太重要了。但这也更是我们应该在审美评价时格外谨慎的原因。如果本书有一点重要启示的话，那就是我们所有人都需要更多的审美谦逊。

索　引

（条目后的数字为原书页码，
见本书边码）

105

美学

索引

美
学

Bence Nanay

AESTHETICS

A Very Short Introduction

Contents

Acknowledgements

I am grateful for the comments on earlier versions of this book
from Nicolas Alzetta, Alma Barner, Felicitas Becker, Constant
Bonard, Chiara Brozzo, Denis Buehler, Patrick Butlin, Dan
Cavedon-Taylor, Will Davies, Ryan Doran, Peter Fazekas, Gabriele
Ferretti, Loraine Gerardin-Laverge, Kris Goffin, Laura Gow, John
Holliday, Anna Ichino, Laszlo Koszeghy, Magdalini Koukou,
Robbie Kubala, Kevin Lande, Jason Leddington, Hans Maes,
Manolo Martinez, Mohan Matthen, Chris McCarroll, Regina-Nina
Mion, Thomas Raleigh, Sam Rose, Maarten Steenhagen, Jakub
Stejskal, Lu Teng, Gerardo Viera, Allert Van Westen, Dan
Williams, Nick Wiltsher and Nick Young and an anonymous
referee. Special thanks to Dominic Lopes, who read three
different versions of the manuscript. The writing of this book was
supported by the ERC Consolidator grant [726251], the FWO
Odysseus grant [G.0020.12N] and the FWO research grant
[G0C7416N].

List of illustrations

Constantin Brancusi, Maiastra, 1912
(?), Brass on limestone base, 28 ¾ × 7
7/8 × 7 7/8 inches (73 × 20 × 20 cm)
overall, The Solomon R. Guggenheim
Foundation, Peggy Guggenheim
Collection, Venice, 1976, 76.2553.50,
Photo: David Heald © The Solomon
R. Guggenheim Foundation, New York.

Aesthetics

Chapter 1
Lost in the museum

You go to the museum. Stand in line for half an hour. Pay 20 bucks. And then, you're there, looking at the exhibited artworks, but you get nothing out of it. You try hard. You read the labels next to the artworks. Even get the audio guide. Still nothing. What do you do?

Maybe you are just not very much into this specific artist. Or maybe you're not that much into paintings in general. Or art. But on other occasions you did enjoy looking at art. And even looking at paintings by this very artist. Maybe even the very same ones. But today, for some reason, it's not happening.

Sounds familiar? We've all struggled with this. Maybe not in the museum, but in the concert hall, or when we're trying to read a novel before going to sleep. Engagement with art can be immensely rewarding, but it can also go wrong very easily. And the line between the two can be very thin.

I use this example to introduce the topic of aesthetics because what we are trying to have in these situations is a kind of experience that this book is about. And not being able to have it (but trying to do so) really pins down what these experiences are and how important they are for all of us.

While I have used examples from art, this can also happen when we are trying to take in the view from a mountaintop or when we are trying to savour a gourmet meal in vain. Aesthetic engagement (with art, nature, or food) can be a bumpy ride.

Non-elitist aesthetics

Aesthetics is about some special kinds of experiences. Ones we care about a lot. The Greek word '*aesthesis*' means 'perception' and when the German philosopher, Alexander Baumgarten (1714–62) introduced the concept of 'aesthetics' in 1750, what he meant by it was precisely the study of sensory experiences (*scientia cognitionis sensitivae*).

The experiences that aesthetics talks about come on a spectrum. We care about some experiences more than others. Not just the experience of artworks in a museum or of an opera performance. Also the experience of the autumn leaves in the park on our way home from work or even just the light of the setting sun falling on the kitchen table. But aesthetics is also about your experience when you choose the shirt you're going to wear today or when you wonder whether you should put more pepper in the soup. Aesthetics is everywhere. It is one of the most important aspects of our life.

Aesthetics is sometimes considered to be too elitist—by artists, musicians, even by philosophers. This is based on a misunderstanding of the subject, something this book aims to correct. So-called 'high art' has no more claim on aesthetics than sitcoms, tattoos, or punk rock. And the scope of aesthetics is far wider than that of art, high or low. It includes much of what we care about in life.

Witold Gombrowicz (1904–69), the Polish avant-garde novelist, captured this sentiment very elegantly:

The food does not always taste best in first-class restaurants. To me, art almost always speaks more forcefully when it appears in an imperfect, accidental, and fragmentary way, somehow just signaling its presence, allowing one to feel it through the ineptitude of the interpretation. I prefer the Chopin that reaches me in the street from an open window to the Chopin served in great style from the concert stage.

It is not the job of aesthetics to tell you which artworks are good and which ones are bad. Nor is it the job of aesthetics to tell you what experiences are worth having—Chopin in the street or Chopin in the concert hall. If an experience is worth having for you, it thereby becomes a potential subject of aesthetics. You can get your aesthetic kicks where you find them. Aesthetics is not a field guide that tells you which experiences are allowed and which are not. It is not a map that helps you find them either. Aesthetics is a way of analysing what it means to have these experiences. Aesthetics is, and should be, completely non-judgemental.

Here is an evocative example. Fernand Léger (1881–1955), the French painter, describes how he and his friend observed a tailor's shop owner arranging seventeen waistcoats, with corresponding cufflinks and neckties, in the display window. The tailor spent eleven minutes on each waistcoat. He moved it to the left by a couple of millimetres, then went outside, in front of the shop, to take a look. Then went back in, moved it to the right a bit, and so on. He was so absorbed that he didn't even notice that Léger and his friend were watching him. Léger was left somewhat humiliated, pondering how few painters take as much aesthetic interest in their work as this old tailor. And surely even fewer museum-goers. Léger's point, and also the guiding principle of this book, is that the tailor's experience is as worthy of being called aesthetic as any museum-goer's admiring Léger's paintings.

3

Thinking about aesthetics in this inclusive way opens up new ways of understanding old questions about the social aspect of our aesthetic engagements and the importance of aesthetic values for our own self. It also makes it possible to think about art and aesthetics in a genuinely global manner that does not presuppose the primacy of the 'West'.

Aesthetics or philosophy of art?

Aesthetics is not the same as philosophy of art. Philosophy of art is about art. Aesthetics is about many things—including art. But it is also about our experience of breathtaking landscapes or the pattern of shadows on the wall opposite your office.

This book is about aesthetics. As a result, it is both broader and narrower in scope than a book about philosophy of art would be. Philosophy of art talks about a wide variety of philosophical questions concerning art—metaphysical, linguistic, political, ethical questions. I will not touch most of these questions. There will be no talk of the definition of art for example, of how artworks are different from all the other objects in the world.

Barnett Newman (1905–70), the American abstract painter, famously said that aesthetics is as irrelevant for artists as ornithology is for birds. It should be clear that it is philosophy of art that would be the equivalent of ornithology in this blatant provocation—and not aesthetics. It is philosophy of art that is in the business of categorizing artworks and mulling over differences between different species/genres, not aesthetics. So Newman's quip is really about philosophy of art, not aesthetics. Aesthetics, the study of the very experiences artists are working with and are trying to evoke, is very relevant to each and every artist.

But, of course, artworks can trigger all kinds of experiences and aesthetics does not even talk about all of these. I'm sure an art thief has some kind of experience of the artwork she steals, but this is unlikely to be the kind of experience this book is about. Or imagine that I promise to give you a lot of money if you run through the entire Metropolitan Museum of Art and count how many of the paintings are signed. I'm sure you could do it, but this does not exactly put you in an aesthetic state of mind, however broadly one understands that.

We engage aesthetically with artworks, but we engage with artworks in all kinds of other ways as well. And there are many other things we aesthetically engage with. (Throughout the book I use 'aesthetic experience' and 'aesthetic engagement' more or less interchangeably, acknowledging that aesthetic engagement is something we do and aesthetic experience is what we feel while we are engaging aesthetically.) Art and aesthetics come apart. But this does not mean that we should ignore the connection altogether. Many of our aesthetically valuable moments come from engaging with art.

In other words, art is an important object of aesthetics, but it is by no means privileged. According to an influential strand in 'Western' aesthetics, our aesthetic engagement with art—actually, with high art—is just completely different from our aesthetic engagement with anything else. Not only does this line of thought undersell aesthetics inasmuch as it restricts the importance and relevance of aesthetic moments in our life, but it goes against almost all non-'Western' aesthetic traditions. And this book is a very short introduction to aesthetics. Not a very short introduction to one very specific, albeit historically important, aesthetic tradition—the 'Western' one.

Non-'Western' aesthetics

Artefacts have been made everywhere in the world. Music too. Stories as well. Nonetheless, when you go into almost any major art museum in the world, you are likely to encounter objects made in the 'West' (Europe and, if it's a museum of modern art, maybe also North America—I will use scare-quotes around 'West' throughout the book to indicate that the 'West' is obviously not a unitary concept). If you are looking for objects from other parts of the world, you often need to go to a far-away wing or sometimes even to a different museum. But art is not a 'Western' monopoly, and neither is aesthetics.

People have been theorizing about our experience of art all over the world. Sticking to the European line on aesthetics would be as biased as exhibiting only European artworks in a museum. Islamic, Japanese, Chinese, Indonesian, African, Sumer-Assyrian, Pre-Columbian, Sanskrit, and Balinese aesthetics are all incredibly sophisticated thought systems full of very important observations about experiences of art and other things. No book on aesthetics should ignore them.

In fact, it is 'Western' aesthetics that is, in many ways, the outlier—with its emphasis (or should I say obsession?) on judging, on high art, and on taking aesthetic engagement out of its social contexts. I am not going to pretend to cover all aesthetic traditions in this book. But neither will I focus on uniquely 'Western' ideas that blatantly fail to resonate with the rest of the world, regardless of the prestige of the dead white males who came up with them.

Chapter 2
Sex, drugs, and rock 'n' roll

The experiences that would count as aesthetic in some sense are a diverse bunch. Not just listening to your favourite song or seeing your favourite film. But also watching a 'greatest goals' compilation on YouTube, finally deciding on a pair of shoes, choosing where exactly to put the coffee maker on a kitchen counter. It is quite a challenge to find something these all have in common.

And of course one should not be too inclusive. Philosophers often contrast the experience of art with drug-induced and sexually charged experiences (and also with hedonistic experiences in general, like heavy partying, that the term 'rock 'n' roll' is supposed to capture). So the traditional way of thinking about aesthetics is that we have to somehow draw a line between the aesthetic and the non-aesthetic so that sex and drugs are out, but hairstyle and music are in. How can this be done?

I use this sex, drugs, and rock 'n' roll problem as a backdrop to introducing the most important approaches to aesthetics. I don't actually think that we can maintain a distinction between aesthetic experiences on the one hand and sex, drugs, and rock 'n' roll on the other. All things can be experienced in an aesthetic manner and some drug-induced experiences, for example, could very much count as aesthetic. But going through these approaches to aesthetics helps us to see just how difficult it is to keep the aesthetic and the non-aesthetic apart.

I will talk about four influential accounts of aesthetics, focusing on beauty, pleasure, emotion, and 'valuing for its own sake'. Not just to dismiss them or to show that they are not working. Not to make fun of them either. I'm talking about them because each and every one of them contains some really important pointers to how we should and how we should not think about the domain of aesthetics.

Beauty?

The most widely shared take on aesthetics is that it's about beauty. Just look around in the street—the word 'aesthetics' routinely shows up in beauty salons. And it is tempting to take something like a beauty-salon approach when trying to explain what aesthetics, the philosophical discipline, is about. The general thought is that some things are beautiful, others are not. Aesthetics helps us to keep them apart, and maybe even explain why beautiful things are beautiful.

I call this the 'beauty-salon approach' because in cosmetic surgery or the nail business there are fairly clear conceptions of what is beautiful and what is not. In fact, the main aim is to turn something not-so-beautiful into something more beautiful. And many of those who think that aesthetics is about beauty work with similar assumptions about a division line in the world between those things that are beautiful and those that are not.

The beauty-salon approach solves the sex, drugs, and rock 'n' roll problem with little effort. Aesthetic experiences are experiences of beautiful things. Drug-induced experiences or sexual experiences, or the experience of rock 'n' roll, are not of beautiful things. So they won't count as aesthetic.

It would be too easy to mock this view for its moralizing and judgemental overtones (rock 'n' roll is the devil's music and marijuana is the devil's harvest, and sex is, well, sex), but it is important that the real problem with the beauty-salon approach is not that it draws the division line between the beautiful and the non-beautiful in an elitist or prudish manner. The real problem is that it draws any such division line.

Being beautiful is very different from, say, being red. We can sort all the things in the world into two piles: red things and non-red things. This may not make a lot of sense, but we could do it. But we can't sort all the things in the world into the pile of the beautiful things and the other, non-beautiful pile. At least not if we want beauty to have anything to do with aesthetics. As Oscar Wilde (1854–1900) says, 'no object is so ugly that, under certain conditions of light and shade, or proximity to other things, it will not look beautiful; no object is so beautiful that, under certain conditions, it will not look ugly'.

The point is that beauty is not a feature of objects that remains the same at all times, in all contexts, for all observers. If this concept is to be even remotely useful in aesthetics, it needs to be able to capture the fleeting nature of beauty and the fact that, as Oscar Wilde rightly noted, we sometimes see an object as beautiful and sometimes we don't. This has nothing to do with the debate about whether beauty is in the eye of the beholder—something I will come back to in Chapter 5. Even if beauty is not in the eye of the beholder—even if it is 'objective' in some sense, it is highly sensitive to what context we encounter it in. The beauty-salon approach can't explain this context-sensitivity.

Although the beauty-salon approach has dominated much of the history of 'Western' aesthetics, it is not the only approach when it comes to beauty. Here is an alternative, summarized as this pithy slogan, wrongly (but consistently) attributed to Confucius

(551 BCE–479 BCE): 'Everything has beauty but not everyone sees it.' We don't get two piles then, one for beautiful things and one for non-beautiful things. We only get one pile.

Various streaks of avant-garde also endorsed versions of this view. To return to Léger, he also argues against any kind of 'hierarchies of beauty'. Here is an evocative quote by him:

> Beauty is everywhere: perhaps more in the arrangement of your saucepans on the white walls of your kitchen than in your eighteenth-century living room or in the official museum.

The view then is that anything can appear beautiful and aesthetics is exactly about these beautiful experiences. But what makes an experience aesthetic is not that the thing we experience is beautiful, but that we experience it in a certain way (we experience whatever we experience as beautiful). It's not what we experience but rather the way we experience.

This approach captures the anti-elitist and non-judgemental sentiment that I started out with, but there is a sleight of hand here. This way of connecting beauty and aesthetics in fact makes the concept of beauty superfluous. We can tell this story without talking about beauty at all. Beauty is merely a placeholder for the character of our experience—and not a very helpful placeholder either. If aesthetics is about experiencing things, whatever things, as beautiful, then we would want to know what this means. How do I do that? I'm looking at a painting in the museum and my experience is anything but aesthetic. How do I make it into an aesthetic experience? Experience it as beautiful? This is not very helpful advice.

The beauty-salon approach at least gave us a way of making a distinction between aesthetic experiences and non-aesthetic ones (like, allegedly, experiences of sex, drugs, and rock 'n' roll). Not a very good way, but a way nonetheless. The more democratic approach I connected with Confucius and Léger does not, in itself, tell us much about aesthetic experiences. If we go down this route, we still have a lot of explaining to do about what makes some experiences (but not others) the experiences of something as beautiful. And if we can explain this, then any reference to 'beauty' in all this will merely be a not so helpful label.

Nonetheless, the democratic version of the beauty account has taught us something really important. It's not that some things are aesthetic and some others are not. All things (well, almost all things) can trigger aesthetic engagement. And there is nothing, not even the greatest artwork, that will always do so. The big question is how we can explain this kind of aesthetic engagement and the way it is triggered. You can use the label 'experiencing it as beautiful' as a helpful reminder of what this experience is like. But that is not an explanation of this experience.

We can experience the very same object as beautiful and as not beautiful. The former is an aesthetic experience, the latter is not. And the beauty account owes us an explanation of exactly this difference. This explanation will presumably have to do with the way this experience unfolds, or maybe with the way our attention or emotions are exercised. But it has little to do with beauty.

Pleasure?

Another important concept that is often used when talking about the difference between the aesthetic and the non-aesthetic is pleasure. The general thought is that aesthetics is about pleasure. The non-aesthetic is not. Aesthetic experiences are (often—clearly not always) pleasurable experiences—that's why we like having them. The hope is that we can understand what makes an experience aesthetic if we understand the pleasure it involves.

Not all pleasure is aesthetic. Immanuel Kant (1724–1804) argued at length that what is distinctive of aesthetic pleasure is that it is disinterested. And millions of pages were written about just what this 'disinterested pleasure' might mean. Instead of doing more Kant scholarship, I want to start with the psychology of pleasure.

Psychologists make a distinction between two kinds of pleasure. The first kind of pleasure is what you feel when something unpleasant stops. I will call it 'relief pleasure' because it is triggered by the body's returning to its normal state after a period of perturbation. So if you're ravenously hungry and finally get to eat something, the pleasure you feel is relief pleasure—your body returns to its pre-hunger normal state.

Relief pleasure is short-lived. We're done with the unpleasant things—the pleasure marks the moment of relief. But it's only a moment. And relief pleasure does not motivate. It may be the consequence of something we do, but it does not make us do further things.

Contrast this with what I will call 'sustaining pleasure'. Sustaining pleasure motivates us to keep on doing what we are doing—it sustains our activity. We're walking along the beach and it's very pleasurable. It's not a relief from anything. It just feels good. It can go on for a long time—unlike relief pleasure. And it motivates us to keep on walking.

As the Canadian philosopher Mohan Matthen (1948–), building on these psychological distinctions, points out, one and the same activity can give you relief pleasure in some contexts and sustaining pleasure in another. Eating is a good example. It can give you relief pleasure when you have the first bite after not eating for a day. But it can also give you sustaining pleasure if you are enjoying a gourmet meal.

Aesthetic pleasure is typically sustaining pleasure. You are looking at a painting, and the pleasure you feel motivates you to keep on looking at it. It is an open-ended activity just as walking along the beach is. Our pleasure sustains our continued engagement with the painting. It is sometimes even difficult to tear ourselves away.

This gives us a complicated picture concerning the sex, drugs, and rock 'n' roll problem. Some sexual and drug-induced activities will give us sustaining pleasure. So we can't just reject sex and drugs wholesale and exclude them from the elite circle of aesthetic activities. I think this is an advantage of the account—I don't see why some sexual and drug-induced experiences could not count as aesthetic. And the pleasure account even gives us a pointer about what it is that makes some but not other sexual and drug-induced experiences qualify, namely, sustaining pleasure.

There is a fair amount of psychological research on how sustaining pleasure motivates and helps the ongoing activity. One example is drinking. If you drink a largish amount of a kind of beverage you like, this can lead to sustaining pleasure. You take pleasure in taking a sip, maybe swirling it around your mouth, swallowing, taking another sip, and so on. There is a certain rhythm to it and the pleasure you take in this activity sustains this rhythm, but also fine-tunes it.

We know a lot about the physiological mechanisms involved in this in the case of drinking—how the synchronizing of the working of various muscles leads to the seamless coordination of the processes involved in drinking. But how does it happen in the case of aesthetic engagement? What would be the equivalent of the working of our neck-muscles? No muscles are directly involved in most aesthetic engagement, after all.

Sustaining pleasure motivates and fine-tunes our ongoing aesthetic engagement by means of controlling our attention. No muscles are directly involved in most aesthetic engagement, but attention is very much involved. When you are looking at that painting, the pleasure you take in doing so nudges your attention to keep on engaging. So the account of aesthetic pleasure as sustaining pleasure owes us an account of how our attention is exercised in our aesthetic engagement.

One important reason why we should really clarify what kind of attention is sustained by sustaining pleasure comes from feminist film theory. The British film theorist Laura Mulvey (1941–) argues in her extremely influential essay 'Visual Pleasure and Narrative Cinema' that mainstream films almost always try to trigger 'visual pleasures' that are typically the male visual pleasures of voyeurism. The main protagonist the audience is encouraged to identify with tends to be male and we are often encouraged to see the women who show up in these films through the eyes of this male protagonist. This highly sexualized 'male gaze' as Mulvey calls it is what constitutes the visual pleasure of narrative cinema.

This 'visual pleasure' is sustaining pleasure by any account (it encourages us to keep on looking), but it is clearly very different from the kind of disinterested aesthetic pleasure aesthetics talks about. So the pleasure account really needs to say more in order to keep aesthetic and non-aesthetic pleasures apart. And, again, a big part of this explanation will have to do with the mental activity that the pleasure maintains, which will have a lot to do with what we are attending to (and how we do so).

Emotions?

The third approach to delineating the aesthetic domain focuses on emotions. The general thought is that aesthetic experiences are emotional experiences. So understanding what makes aesthetic experiences different from other kinds of experiences would be to understand what kind of emotion is triggered here.

Iris Murdoch (1919–99), the Irish novelist, took literature (and art in general) to be 'a sort of disciplined technique for arousing certain emotions'. And George Kubler (1912–96), one of the most influential art historians of the last century, said that one simple way of thinking about art would be as 'an object made for emotional experience'. As a sociological assessment about art, this may have sounded more convincing in 1959, when Kubler wrote it, than in 2019. After all, much of contemporary art tries to stay as far away from our emotions as possible, preferring a merely intellectual or sometimes a merely perceptual engagement (as in the case of conceptual art and op art). But if we take Murdoch's and Kubler's claims to be about aesthetic engagement and not about art, then it amounts to taking aesthetic experiences to be emotional experiences.

The question is: what kinds of emotions are involved? Always the same kind of emotion in all aesthetic engagement? Or different emotions, depending on what we are engaging with and how we do so?

The more extreme view is that it is always the same emotion that we have in all cases of aesthetic engagement. If we have that emotion, it is an aesthetic engagement, if we don't it's not. But what would this 'aesthetic emotion' be? There is no shortage of candidates, from wonder and being moved to the contemplation of formal features. But it is easy to come up with examples of aesthetic engagement where none of these emotions are present.

One striking feature of aesthetic engagements is their diversity: our aesthetic experience of the Grand Canyon and of a Billie Holiday song would involve very different emotions. Looking for just one catch-all emotion that we would have in all these cases would amount to ignoring or papering over the diversity of aesthetics.

And even the same object can trigger very different emotions in different circumstances. One of the weirdest stories I have heard about art was from a very good friend of mine who went to the San Francisco Museum of Modern Art after every first date and sat down in front of a very big Mark Rothko painting to figure out

15

how she felt about the new potential romantic partner. It was not just an environment to think about someone, it was her reaction to the painting that was coloured by the previous encounter. The emotions this large abstract painting evoked on these occasions, I was told, were very different. If aesthetic experience of one painting can lead to such diverse emotions, how could all aesthetic engagement be brought under the umbrella of just one kind of special 'aesthetic emotion'?

Nonetheless, it is undeniable that aesthetic engagement can be, and often is, an emotional affair. Art can make you cry. And nature too. The link between aesthetics and emotions is something all aesthetic traditions, from Islamic and Sanskrit to Japanese and Chinese aesthetics, talk about.

Any account of aesthetic experiences would need to take emotions seriously. But this does not mean that emotions are the make-or-break conditions for having an aesthetic experience. Is only aesthetic engagement emotional? Clearly not. Sex, drugs, and rock 'n' roll can be very emotional—maybe even more so than some of the aesthetic examples I have been using. And it could be argued that almost everything we do is emotion-infused in some sense. So the emphasis on emotions will not be too helpful when looking for what is special about the aesthetic.

Conversely, is aesthetic engagement always emotional? When Fernando Pessoa (1888–1935), the Portuguese poet and writer, describes his aesthetic experience as 'drifting without thoughts or emotions, attending only to my senses', this sounds like a familiar form of aesthetic engagement where emotions take the back seat. In at least some cases of aesthetic experience, it is the sensory that dominates, not the emotional.

Even the contemplation of formal features, one of the alleged examples for 'aesthetic emotions', could be thought to be a perceptual and not an emotional affair. Susan Sontag (1933–2004), the American art critic, for example, characterizes aesthetic experience as 'detached, restful, contemplative, emotionally free, beyond indignation and approval'.

Emotion may not be what makes aesthetic experiences aesthetic. But the emotion accounts of aesthetics are still important inasmuch as they highlight just how emotions can be a crucial part of aesthetic experiences. Any account of aesthetics needs to tell a story about how emotional and aesthetic experiences can be, and often are, intertwined.

For its own sake?

Susan Sontag talks about aesthetic experience as detached. Detached not just from emotions, but from indignation, approval, and also practical considerations. And this is the last popular candidate for keeping the aesthetic and the non-aesthetic apart: aesthetic engagement is engagement for its own sake. We don't do it in order to achieve some other, further goal. We do it just for the aesthetic kicks.

This proposal comes in many flavours. Some talk about valuing for its own sake: when we have an aesthetic experience, we value what we are experiencing (or maybe the experience itself) for its own sake. I will not say much about this line of reasoning, because I am not even sure that we are valuing anything when we have aesthetic experiences, let alone valuing things for their own sake. In any case, that would depend on one's account of value and I am definitely not opening that can of worms here. What do I value when I gaze at the specks of dust dancing in a beam of sunshine? The specks of dust? Or am I valuing my own experience? What does it even mean to value one's own experience? That I like to have it? Giving it a thumbs up? If we can formulate the 'for its own sake' account without relying on the concept of valuing, we really should try to do so.

But we can avoid talking about values and focus on just why we are doing what we are doing when engaging aesthetically. Are we trying to achieve something else or are we doing it only for its own sake? If I read a novel so that I can pass a test in my literature class, I do one thing (read the novel) in order to achieve something else (pass the test). If I read it for just reading it, that's closer to the aesthetic domain. But the aesthetic experience can kick in even though I started reading it because of the literature class. In that case, I am not doing it *purely* for its own sake, but I am nonetheless engaging with it aesthetically. And that doesn't mean that my engagement is necessarily less aesthetic. These intermediate cases show that 'doing it for its own sake' is not the holy grail of aesthetics.

Here is another way to capture the 'for its own sake' intuition. Some activities only make sense if they reach an end point or a goal. They are done in order to achieve something. They should be completed. You can't do them just a little bit. Like running a marathon in under four hours.

With activities of this kind, there are two options. You either achieve the goal or you don't. If you don't, then your frustrated desires lead to even stronger desires that are also likely to be frustrated. If you do, well, then four hours is for losers and 3.45 is the new goal. Then 3.30. And so on. There is always a higher mountain to climb.

Luckily not all activities are like this. Some other activities you can do just a little bit. They make sense even if you don't complete them. They are not done to achieve a goal. Like running for the sake of running.

Some things you do for the trophy; some things for the process itself. We need both. Very few people have jobs where we can just enjoy the process of whatever we are doing without any pressure to achieve anything. There are always goals, deadlines, promotion criteria.

And even in our free time much of what we do is geared towards some very specific goal. We cook a meal with the ultimate purpose to serve it to our friends, not just cook aimlessly. So we can't avoid activities we do for the achievement. But we need a healthy balance between activities we do for achievements and activities we do for the process itself.

Aesthetic engagement is not a trophy activity. It is, if it goes well, a process activity. You don't do it for the trophy. It makes sense to do it even though you don't follow it through to its goal or end point, because it has no goal or end point. You can look at a painting for just a little bit. This activity has no natural (or unnatural) end point. Aesthetic engagement is an open-ended activity.

Any account of aesthetic engagement needs to explain this important feature: that it is open-ended and a process, not a trophy activity. But this won't be the cut-off mark that divides the aesthetic from the non-aesthetic either. I have been focusing on examples like looking at a painting, where there really is no end point to the activity. But in other examples of aesthetic engagements, there is an end point. Sonatas and films have a very natural end point, namely, when they are over. We can think about them after they are over, but in some very important sense, there is an end point to the experience itself. These aesthetic activities are very much unlike the timeless contemplation of paintings in this respect.

So while the process activity is an important aspect of some cases of aesthetic engagement, it is not a universal feature of all aesthetic engagement. We could make a distinction *within* the category of aesthetic engagements—some of them are goal-directed, some others are not. But the lack of goal-directedness is not what defines this category.

Where does this leave us with the sex, drugs, and rock 'n' roll issue? As in the case of the pleasure-centred account, the emphasis on doing things for their own sake also divides up the category of sexual and drug-induced experiences. Aldous Huxley (1894–1963) wrote an entire book about how his own drug-induced experiences were detached in exactly the way aesthetic experiences are detached. Again, I take this to be the right approach to sex and drugs—some of these should be part of the domain of aesthetics. Nonetheless, the four standard approaches to aesthetics still failed to give us a clear account of where exactly this domain starts and where it ends.

The 'for its own sake' account clearly captures an important aspect of aesthetic experiences, but this is not the only important aspect. Whatever the final account of the distinction between aesthetic and non-aesthetic will be, it needs to capture the importance of doing things in an open-ended way for their own sake.

Attention?

What we have learned from accounts of beauty is that if we set the beauty-salon approach aside, aesthetics is often about experiencing things as beautiful, where 'as beautiful' is a placeholder for some character of our experiences, which needs to be filled in by any account of aesthetics. Emotion-centred accounts highlight the importance of emotions in our experience, but it still needs to be worked out just how aesthetic experiences are coloured by emotions.

The pleasure-based accounts emphasized the importance of sustaining pleasure, but they are incomplete if they fail to specify what form of attention is involved in such sustaining pleasure. And the 'for its own sake' accounts, as long as we ditch the concept of valuing, push the importance of open-ended, detached, process activities.

I will argue that these accounts all point in the same direction, namely, that what is special about aesthetics is the way we exercise our attention in aesthetic experiences. This can help us explain how experiencing something as beautiful qualifies as aesthetic and also what makes these experiences emotionally infused. Attention was the missing piece in the pleasure-based accounts and talking about the detached open-ended exercise of attention captures much of the 'for its own sake' accounts. As Marcel Proust (1871–1922) said, 'Attention can take various forms and the job of the artist is to evoke the most superior of these.'

Chapter 3
Experience and attention

What all things aesthetic have in common is something very simple: the way you're exercising your attention. This can also happen if this experience is drug-induced or sexually charged (or both). And it often does not happen even when you are staring at a masterpiece.

The difference attention makes

Remember *Goldfinger*? It was one of the better James Bond films (made in 1964). This is the one where the gold-obsessed villain, Auric Goldfinger, schemes to blow up the entire federal gold reserve in Fort Knox. Here he is (Figure 1).

It's an old film, but if you've seen it recently, say, in the last couple of years, it's impossible not to notice the uncanny resemblance between the look of the villain Goldfinger and, well, the 45th president of the US (Figure 2).

Once you've seen this similarity, it's very difficult to unsee it. And it really messes with your mind when you watch the movie, especially given that Goldfinger blows up the federal gold reserve in order to increase the value of his own gold holdings. For me, at least, this now takes a lot away from the enjoyment of the film.

1. Auric Goldfinger, the main villain of the James Bond movie *Goldfinger* (1964).

2. Donald J. Trump, the 45th president of the United States of America.

Attending to the similarity between Goldfinger and Donald J. Trump can make a huge difference. It can change your experience in an aesthetically significant way. This highlights the importance of which features of the artwork we pay attention to. Paying attention to an irrelevant feature could and would derail our experience.

In this example, the aesthetic difference this shift of attention triggers is likely to be a negative one. But it doesn't have to be.

Attending to a relevant feature can completely transform your experience, as in the case of a 16th-century Flemish landscape painting by Bruegel (Figure 3). It's half landscape, half seascape, a nice diagonal composition, with the peasant at the centre ploughing a field with great concentration. A quaint everyday scene; nothing very dramatic. Until you read the title: *The Fall of Icarus.*

What? Where is Icarus? I don't see anyone falling. What does this peasant have to do with that dramatic mythological event? You scan the picture for some trace of Icarus and then you find him (or at least his legs, as he's just fallen into the water) just below the large ship tucked away in the bottom right corner.

My guess is that your experience is now very different. While the part of the canvas where Icarus's legs are depicted was not a particularly salient feature of your experience of the painting before (perhaps you didn't even glance at it), now everything else in the picture seems to be somehow connected to it.

Maybe you experienced the picture as disorganized before, but attending to Icarus's legs pulls the picture together. (This, in any case, seems to be the effect Bruegel was aiming for almost 500 years ago.)

Here is another example, this time involving music. In music it can make a huge difference whether you're attending to the bass

3. Pieter Bruegel the Elder, *The Fall of Icarus* (c.1555), Royal Museums of Fine Art, Brussels.

or the melody. But there are cases where this difference is even more salient. The first canon in Johann Sebastian Bach's *A Musical Offering* (1747) is a fugue-like piece for two instruments. But there is a twist: the two instruments play the very same melody—one from beginning to end, the other backwards, starting at the end and moving backwards.

This is difficult to spot without seeing the music sheet. However, once you have noticed it, it's impossible not to pay attention to this feature of the music. And this is exactly why Bach wrote this piece—to show off the extent of his skill. Attending to this feature is likely to make a positive aesthetic difference.

Here's a somewhat less elitist example from the sitcom *How I Met Your Mother* (CBS, 2005–14). Much of the nine seasons and more than 200 episodes of this sitcom was about the complicated romance and wedding of the dream-couple Barney and Robin. The last season was dedicated in its entirety to their wedding. But then (spoiler alert!) came the very last episode and the very last two minutes of the finale, where the showrunners decided to break up the dream-couple and get Robin back together with Ted.

The fans were outraged. This finale was voted the worst moment of television that year. This twist at the very end made many hardcore *How I Met Your Mother* fans burn all their merchandise and memorabilia, but it also achieved something else. If you manage to get yourself to watch the entire nine seasons again, it is difficult not to see the unfolding story very differently. Moments between Ted and Robin will grab your attention much more easily. And you attend to the dynamics between the three characters very differently from the way you did when you had no idea that this would be the ending.

This trick has been widely used in feature films. One way of getting the audience to spend even more money on a film is to get them to watch it again. And films of certain aspirations do this by revealing something at the very end that changes everything, so much so that, seeing the film for the second time, knowing what you know now, will be a very different experience. Christopher Nolan's *Memento* (2000) and *Inception* (2010) are famous examples, but there are many others. You have very little idea what's going on until the end. And when you see these films for the second time, you see them very differently, because you attend to very different features of the story.

Here is another example, this time not involving art. It is about the worst meal I've ever had. My wife was about to give birth to our first child. I drove her to the hospital in a hurry and then had to go back to pick up all the many things necessary for the hospital stay. I was starving, but I obviously wanted to rush back as soon as I could. So I stuck some leftover Chinese food into the microwave while I was packing the bag. Then the food was way too hot, but I had no time to let it cool down, so I forced it down, burning my mouth quite badly. Not a great culinary experience. But I was out of the house in three minutes!

I said it was 'some leftover Chinese food', but in fact it was the doggy bag from the best Chinese restaurant in town, where we had dinner the night before—really excellent food. I wouldn't say it was the best meal I've ever had, but it was a pretty good meal. Not so much the day after. But then what was the difference? The obvious answer is that it was a difference in attention. There were lots of things I was attending to while feverishly stuffing diapers and swaddling clothes into a suitcase, but the food was not among them.

What you are attending to makes a huge difference to your experience in general. And it also makes a huge difference to your experience of artworks. It can completely ruin your experience, as will happen when you watch *Goldfinger* next time (sorry about that!). Or it can make your experience even more rewarding. And in some cases, it can directly confront you with how differently the same artwork appears to you depending on what you're attending to.

But then the question of attention becomes extremely important for anyone interested in aesthetics. Not just for academic philosophers and art historians—for everyone. Imagine that you are sitting in a museum, trying to make sense of the artwork in front of you. What is it that you're supposed to pay attention to? The artwork in front of you has lots of features; it was made by an artist who, no doubt, had a lot of things to say about it. Are you supposed to pay attention to those features of the artwork that the artist found important? Or are you just supposed to pay attention to what the audio guide tells you to?

When we engage with an artwork, we invariably ignore some of its features and focus our attention on others. We ignore the cracks in the paint and focus our attention on other features of the painting's surface; we abstract away from the cracks. When looking at a Romanesque church that was rebuilt in the Baroque era, we may try to ignore the Baroque elements in order to admire the medieval structure. Again, we are attempting to abstract away from some features of the artwork.

But how do we know what features of an artwork we should be paying attention to and what features we should ignore or actively abstract away from? There are no easy answers or cheap shortcuts, I'm afraid. Attention can make or break your aesthetic enjoyment. It can be dangerous—see the *Goldfinger* case—but it can also be, if allocated in the right way, very rewarding aesthetically. We should do more to try to understand what we attend to, and how we do so in aesthetic engagement.

The focus of attention

We know a lot about attention from perceptual psychology and we also know the huge difference it can make to our experience. One of the most celebrated recent experiments about attention demonstrates this nicely. You are shown a short clip of people playing basketball: a team dressed in white against a team dressed in black. Your task is to count how many times the former team passes the ball around. While doing this, more than half of the experimental subjects fail to notice that a man in a gorilla costume walks in the frame, makes funny gestures, spends seven full seconds there, and then leaves. If you're not trying to do any counting tasks, you immediately spot the gorilla. So what you're attending to has serious consequences for whether you spot a man in a gorilla costume bang in the middle of the screen. This phenomenon has a fancy name: 'inattentional blindness'.

Here is a funny and rarely mentioned thing about this experiment: it does not work if you count the number of times the other team—the team dressed in black—passes the ball around. The reason for this is that, well, the gorilla costume is black. If you're attending to the team in white, everything else is noise—the other team, the gym, the gorilla costume. You ignore it; you screen it out.

But when you are attending to the team in black, you will notice the gorilla costume, because it is also black. This should not come as a surprise. When you are trying to flag down a cab, you are seeing every car as either yellow or not yellow (or whatever colour cabs are in your city). The cars that are not yellow are as if they were not there at all. They are noise, to be screened out. Also, when you're looking for Waldo in the *Where is Waldo* books, whatever is not red and white striped is just there to throw you off: you should just ignore it.

Much of our time is spent on attending to some very specific features of what we see and ignoring the rest. When we're trying to do some demanding task, for example, solving the crossword puzzle quickly, there is so much we are trying to ignore so that it does not distract us: anything we smell, hear, and much of what's in our visual field (besides the crossword puzzle). We are natural born ignorers.

And where would we be without this amazing capacity to just shut out much of the world around us? Our mind has limited capacity: if we want to concentrate on something, we need to ignore everything else. And most of the time we do need to concentrate on something: our breakfast, the drive to work, the work itself, and so on.

We understand the psychological mechanisms of how we do this fairly well. Even the earliest stages of our visual processing are highly selective: it only processes information that is relevant in that moment. Everything else is discarded. Some features of the gorilla are discarded as irrelevant for the task at hand as the task only involves attending to what the team in white does and that turns anything black (including the gorilla) into background features.

Your experience depends on what you are attending to. If you shift your attention, your experience will also change. Your experience of the very same concert hall will be very different, depending on whether you are looking for an empty seat or your friend in the crowd. In the former case, all people will melt into the background and the empty seats will pop out. In the latter case, those faces will pop out that are similar to your friend's. Very different experiences indeed.

But how does attention characterize our aesthetic experiences? Here we need to talk not just about *what* we attend to but also about *how* we do so. There are different ways of attending and some of these are more conducive to having (at least some kinds of) aesthetic experiences than others.

Ways of attending

One of the important lessons of the inattentional blindness studies is that whatever we are not attending to just fails to show up in our experience. It is as if we were blind to it. When we did not attend to the gorilla, we did not see the gorilla—we had a fully gorilla-free experience. So not attending to anything entails not having any experience whatsoever.

If you have an amazing meal in a gourmet restaurant, but it is on the occasion of an important business lunch where you really need to impress your boss, you are very unlikely to enjoy the meal. As far as culinary pleasures are concerned, it might as well have been mediocre diner food. Your attention is directed elsewhere, not at the food. Attention is a limited resource: something's gotta give.

One basic distinction vision scientists and psychologists make about attention is that it can be focused or distributed. When you follow the trajectory of five different dots on the screen simultaneously, your attention is distributed. If you are following just one, your attention is focused. These are absolutely routine concepts in psychology when it comes to describing and understanding so-called 'visual search' tasks (tasks like looking for Waldo).

This is a distinction about how many objects we are attending to. But every object has many different features. My coffee cup has colour, shape, weight, and so on. We can attend to one and the same object, but to different features of this object. Attending to the colour of the cup or attending to its weight would give rise to very different experiences. If you shift your attention from the weight of the cup to the colour of the cup, your experience changes. So in the same way that we have a choice about whether we attend to one object or five objects, we also have a choice about whether we attend to one feature of an object or five such features.

So we get not two but four different ways of attending:

(i)   One object, one feature,
(ii) Many objects, one feature,
(iii) Many objects, many features, and
(iv) One object, many features.

This would be nice and logical, but (iii) is not actually an option—this is just not the way our visual system is built. Distributing our attention across five different objects at the same time is tough. In fact, we can only do it for less than a minute even in the most ideal circumstances. After that, we are completely exhausted mentally. And five objects is our absolute limit: we can't do any of this if it is not five, but six different objects. So distributing attention across objects puts a serious strain on the resources, even if it is only one feature we are after. It just doesn't work if we are trying to attend to many features of many objects. We end up losing either some objects or some features from the centre of our attention.

But the other three ways of attending are all very familiar. Take all the objects that are on your kitchen counter. You can pick out one of them, say, a coffee cup, and attend to its colour. This is attending to one and only one feature of one and only one object. You can attend to those objects that happen to be red. That's attending to one and only one feature of many objects. And you can attend to the coffee cup but without zooming in on any particular features.

Attending to one feature of one object happens a lot—each time we are performing some precision task: peeling an apple, for example: only one feature of the apple is interesting here and we will ignore all else (for example, its colour). Attending to one feature of many objects happens even more often: every time we are looking for something, for example.

When I'm looking for a cab, this is exactly what I'm doing. I am looking for exactly one feature of all these cars: whether they are yellow. Running through the airport to catch my flight also involves this way of attending. There are many objects of my attention: all the people and suitcases in my way. But only one feature of these matters to me, namely, how I can get around them. All other features are irrelevant and they are ignored.

I am not attending, for example, to how many of the passengers had a moustache.

What is a bit less common is attending to multiple features of one and the same object. When you are trying to enjoy your very expensive meal in the gourmet restaurant or admiring a painting, you are attending to one thing: the food you're eating and the artwork. But the question is about what features of the food or the painting you are attending to.

So the choice is simple: you can be completely obsessed and preoccupied with one and only one feature of what you see. And sometimes this is what is needed when performing some difficult task. But you can also attend to many features of the very same object. And this is where things get interesting.

Attending to many features of the same object does not guarantee aesthetic experiences. But it is a good starting point. When James Bond is feverishly trying to dismantle a ticking bomb, without having any idea which part is doing what, he is attending to many features of one object. But I doubt that this would be an experience he would want to repeat.

What is also needed is that our attention to the many features of the same object is free and open-ended. What James Bond does is this: he hectically moves around his super-focused attention from one part of the bomb to another, in search of a way to make it stop. He knows exactly what he needs to do, just doesn't know how to do it. He is attending to many features but his attention to all of these features is razor-sharp.

When we have certain kinds of aesthetic experiences, we are doing the exact opposite of this: we are not looking for anything in particular. We are attending to multiple features of the not very unusual scene in front of us, but we are not trying to focus either on any feature in particular or on any group of features. Our attention is free and open-ended.

I have made many distinctions, but there is only one that matters for us now. The distinction between open-ended and not open-ended (or, as I will call it, 'fixated') attention. All open-ended attention is distributed, but not all distributed attention is open-ended—for example, James Bond's isn't. Distributed attention is a good start if we want to have open-ended attention, but it is not enough.

When peeling an apple, our attention is fixated (maybe not the attention of professional apple-peelers, but definitely mine). It is fixated on one feature of one object. This is fixated and focused attention. Our attention is also fixated when we are looking for a cab, only zooming in on one feature of all the cars: the yellow colour. But Bond's attention is also fixated, this time fixated on many features of the bomb. This is fixated and distributed attention. None of these experiences involve open-ended attention and none of them are much fun.

The original distinction from vision science was between focused and distributed attention. But distributed attention is not a guarantee of open-endedness. When you look for a cab, your attention is distributed (across objects), but not open-ended at all. And James Bond's attention is also distributed (across properties), but not open-ended. I reserve the label of 'open-ended attention' to those ways of attending when we distribute our attention among many features of an object, but not with a specific aim or goal in mind.

Fixated attention is exhausting in the long run. Open-ended attention is a form of relaxation for the mind or at least the perceptual system. And our perceptual system really likes a bit of relaxation now and then.

Here is an analogy that may be helpful: working out. You can exercise only your biceps. Obsessively, over and over again. This would be the equivalent of focusing your attention on one feature only. But you can also exercise several muscles at the same time—say, exercising your biceps while being on the treadmill. This would correspond to attending to many features of the same object. But there is nothing open-ended about either of these.

Exercise is good for you, of course, but exercising all day every day is just too much. You also need to relax. And relaxation does not mean being motionless, but, say, leisurely strolling down the street, moving many of your muscles, but none of them too much. Now this would be the equivalent of open-ended attention.

One big difference is this: very few of us exercise all day long. But we do attend in a focused manner most of the time. Otherwise there would be a lot of dropped plates, spilled milk, and traffic accidents. So we need to be extra careful what we do when we do not absolutely have to attend in a focused manner, because these precious moments are rare.

And just as your body needs some downtime when you're not exercising any of your muscles, your perceptual system also needs some downtime, when your attention is not fixated. It would be just plain silly to start exercising a different muscle as soon as you're out of the gym. And it is plain silly to spend those rare moments when we do not need to be fixated on avoiding traffic jams or on trying not to mess up our promotion with more fixated attention. Open-ended attention is the mind's downtime and without it life would be tough.

I'm not saying that aesthetic experience is all about relaxing the perceptual system. But if the perceptual system is overstretched, the aesthetic experience is unlikely to happen. Open-ended attention is special. It allows us to compare two seemingly unrelated shapes in a painting. To trace the way the violin's melody provides a counterpoint to the piano's. Or to attend to the contrasts or parallels between the meal's ingredients. This way of attending is what is special about at least some kinds of aesthetic experiences.

But not all of them. While some aesthetic experiences seem to be open-ended experiences, you may not recognize some of your strongest aesthetic experiences in this characterization at all. Some of your strong aesthetic experiences might involve fixated and even focused attention. Not detachment but strong attachment to what you see. As the French avant-garde film-maker, Danièle Huillet (1936–2006), said: 'We want people to lose themselves in our films. All this talk about "distanciation" is bullsh*t.' I will come to these. But at least some typical aesthetic experiences involve open-ended attention.

The freedom of perception

Attention in many aesthetic contexts is free and open-ended. James Bond's quest to defuse the bomb was neither. He was blatantly not free to attend to any features of the bomb—it would have been stupid to attend to the colour harmony among the wires he was contemplating cutting, for example. And it was very clearly not an open-ended process.

This connection between open-ended attention and freedom is more than a metaphor. When our attention is open-ended, we are not looking for anything specific. We are happy to find what we find, but there is no specific quest to complete. This does not mean that we're not interested. But we just don't have anything specific that we are looking for. Attending in this open-ended manner liberates our perception.

When we are looking at a painting we have never seen before, we often move around our attention among the many features of the work: look here, look there. But we have no clear idea what it is that we're after. If this is a search, it is a search without constraints, without no-go areas. Anything (or almost anything) can be potentially interesting and relevant.

We are incredibly good at ignoring and discounting almost everything we see, so that we can attend to what is important. But when our attention is open-ended, we let ourselves be surprised. It is a much less predictable state than fixated attention and it is this lack of predictability that makes it much more rewarding.

Attending is an action—it is an action we are performing all the time we are awake. And like all other actions, we sometimes perform it freely and sometimes not so freely. Most of the time, not so freely. Most of the time, attention has no-go areas. In fact, the vast majority of areas are no-go areas when our attention is fixated. What we are not fixated on is a mere distraction—it is off limits.

But when our attention is open-ended, it can roam freely. And this freedom also explains many important characteristics of the way attention works in aesthetic contexts. For example, the sad truth is that you can't just count to three and make your attention open-ended at will. In order to try to soften the focus of your attention, making it more open-ended, this act of trying is itself an exercise in fixated attention, which goes against anything open-ended. Trying not to try is not easy to pull off.

Also, open-ended attention needs time. If you're hurried, it's not likely to happen. It's easy to see why. The open-endedness of attention is jeopardized when we are in a rush. We can't let our attention roam freely, because we need to wrap things up in thirty seconds.

Think of attention like butter. It is a limited resource but it can be applied in different ways. It can be spread thinly or thickly. If it is 'spread across a number of potentially interesting features, it is spread so thinly that each such feature gets less. The attention these features get is softer, milder, less piercing. It is so much more enjoyable.

Aesthetic attention

Open-ended attention is an important feature of aesthetic experiences. Is it a make-or-break condition? Very unlikely. It captures what has been a very influential form of aesthetic experience in a very specific time period (roughly, in the last couple of hundred years) in a very specific part of the world (roughly, the 'West'). We have very little evidence about whether people in medieval times went in for open-ended attention and, more crucially, it might be on its way out in our current smartphone-obsessed times, which are not exactly conducive to open-ended attention. As Marina Abramović (1946–), the avant-garde performance artist, said, 'Today, our attention is less than the television advertisement. We're looking at six or seven problems constantly.' That doesn't exactly sound open-ended.

People like Fernando Pessoa, Susan Sontag, or Marcel Proust wrote beautifully about aesthetic experiences where attention is open-ended and it is important to understand what kind of experiences they were talking about. But these are not the only kind of experiences that would count as aesthetic. Nonetheless, taking the role of attention seriously can help us to say something about less open-ended aesthetic experiences as well.

When we have an aesthetic experience, we don't just attend to the object we see. We also attend to the quality of our experience. Importantly, we attend to the relation between the two. Most of the time, we are attending to the objects around us, without any attention to our experience of them. In a traffic jam, I tend to attend to the car in front of me, the traffic light turning red, the pedestrians in my way.

However, we can also attend to how seeing a certain object hits us. This would mean attending to the relation between an object and the quality of our experience of this object. This does not mean that we direct our eyes inward and are completely absorbed by our own experience only. It is important that both the object and the quality of our experience of this object are part of what our attention latches onto.

To use a very prosaic example, when we are looking at an apple, we can attend to the features of the apple. Or we can attend to the features of our experience of the apple. Or we can attend to both, and the relation between the two. Attending this third way is what I take to be a crucial (and maybe even close to universal) feature of aesthetic experience.

Here is an appeal to authority. Fernando Pessoa describes aesthetic experience in very similar terms. As he says, 'true experience consists in reducing one's contact with reality whilst at the same time intensifying one's analysis of that contact'. Intensifying one's analysis of the contact to the experienced object is exactly what I mean by attending to the relation between the experienced object and the quality of our experience.

There are many ways of attending to the relation between the experienced object and the quality of our experience. In much of this chapter I talked about one specific way of achieving this by means of open-ended attention, but it is not the only way. One consequence of open-ended and unrestricted attention is that our attention can roam freely; not just on features of the perceived object, but also on features of our experience.

Choosing your outfit for a first date also involves attending to the quality of your experience: you stop, look in the mirror, see how what you see hits you. A lot else might be going on—you might try to second-guess how your date may react and how their reaction might be different from yours. But whatever you do, it must involve attending to the relation between the object and the quality of your experience of the object.

Similarly, you spend hours climbing to a mountaintop. You finally look around. Sure, you'll attend to the view—the fields and rivers below. But not just that. If that's all you were attending to, it would not have been worth spending all that time on the climb. You will also attend to your own experience, which might be coloured by a sense of accomplishment.

How about Danièle Huillet's insistence that the experience she wants to trigger is one of absorption and not open-endedness or detachment? Absorption does not mean that the experience of what we are absorbed in completely falls out of the picture. When we are absorbed, we are often very much aware of being absorbed—we are enjoying not just what absorbs our attention but also the absorbed experience itself. So it is another way of attending to the relation between what we perceive and the experience of what we perceive.

While the importance of open-ended attention in aesthetic experience might be a specifically 'Western' thing, attending to the relation between the perceived object and the quality of the experience of this object is a theme we can find in a number of non-'Western' aesthetic traditions. One strikingly explicit example is Rasa: the central concept of Sanskrit aesthetics, which influenced thinking about art not only in India, but also in Indonesia and even parts of East Africa.

Rasa is often translated as the savouring of the emotional flavour of our experience. Flavour here is more than a metaphor—the experience of art in this tradition is a multimodal experience addressing all of our sense modalities. But the crucial point for our purposes is in the concept of 'savouring'. Savouring a meal means that you attend to the relation between the contrast and harmony of different experiences. It means attending to how different flavours hit you. In the example of forcing down the leftover Chinese food, this is exactly what was missing. Rasa theory takes something like what I referred to as aesthetic attention to be one of the most important components of our experience of works of art.

But one might wonder whether this would make aesthetic experience too cheap: I can attend to the quality of my experience while I am having my wisdom tooth extracted. I really can. And I can also attend to the relation between the tooth and my pain. But this does not make this experience an aesthetic experience (alas). What is also needed is the open-endedness of this attention.

And now we can put together the pieces of the puzzle about what makes aesthetic experiences aesthetic: the way we exercise our attention. It is a specific exercise of attention that could be described as seeing something as beautiful. And attention can be (but does not have to be) modulated by emotions.

We learned from the 'for its own sake' account about the importance of detachment and open-endedness in the aesthetic domain and we can do justice to this in terms of the free and open-ended attention with few no-go zones. And we have seen that the pleasure account owes us a theory of aesthetic attention—and this is exactly what I have tried to give here.

Finally, it's time to return to the question of sex, drugs, and rock 'n' roll. In the case of many sexual experiences we are attending to the relation between what we perceive and the quality of our experiences and the same goes for drugs (Huxley's vivid description of his peyote trips is all about this). So we have no reason to deny the aesthetic label from these experiences.

A recurring theme in old and by now somewhat stale discussions of perception is that perception is transparent. This just means that we see through our experience in the way we see through a clean window. The classic line is that if you are staring at a tomato and try to attend to your experience of the tomato, you automatically start attending to the tomato itself. So the experience itself is transparent—you look through it.

This may or may not be the case when you look at a tomato because you want to eat it. My claim is that things are very different when it comes to an aesthetic experience of a tomato. In this case, you attend not just to the tomato, but also to the quality of your experience of the tomato. And to the relation between the two. Aesthetic experiences are not transparent.

Chapter 4
Aesthetics and the self

Why do we pay a lot of money to listen to a concert or to buy a book? Why do we spend hours cooking a gourmet meal? And why do we exert a lot of energy to climb to a mountaintop? My answer is that we do all these things in order to have experiences that are important for us personally. These experiences matter for who we are, for who we take ourselves to be.

Just how important? Some recent experimental studies show that most of us consider our taste in music and film to be one of our most essential features. Our taste in food and clothing is not far behind. Imagine that tomorrow you wake up but you're much smarter than you are now. Or much less smart. Would that still be you? Or imagine that you wake up being kinder or skinnier or a Republican or less interested in yoga. Would that still be you?

According to the findings, very few of these compare to the scenario where you wake up and your musical taste is the exact opposite of what it used to be. We tend to consider our taste in music to be a way more important part of who we are than our moral, political, or even religious views.

Changing self, changing aesthetics

Our taste in music, film, and art is super-important for us. And not just that, our taste in what we eat, what kind of coffee we drink, how we dress. We take our aesthetic preferences to be a big part of who we are.

But these preferences change surprisingly quickly and often without us noticing. According to some recent findings aesthetic preferences are the most stable in middle-aged people and they are much more fluid in younger and, somewhat surprisingly, older age groups. But even the aesthetic preferences of people in the most stable age group undergo at least one major change as often as every two weeks in an aesthetic domain they really care about.

We like to think that we don't change much. Or if we do, we are in control of this change. But we are spectacularly wrong about this. We have very little control over how and how much we change.

Take the example of a widely explored psychological phenomenon, the 'mere exposure effect'. The more you are exposed to something, the more you tend to like it. Just the mere exposure to something changes your preferences. And this happens even if you are not aware of what you are exposed to.

The mere exposure effect influences your liking of people, songs, colours, even paintings. In one experiment, a professor of psychology at Cornell put some seemingly random pictures among the slides for an introductory vision science lecture. So in the middle of a lecture on how vision works you suddenly saw a Renoir or Morisot painting, with no explanation given. It was just there as decoration.

While these paintings seemed to come up randomly, they were part of an experiment. Some of them were shown more often than others and at the end of the semester, the students were asked to rate the pictures shown. They systematically rated those that were shown more often more highly than the ones that were shown only once. Very few of these students said that they remembered seeing any of these pictures before.

The mere exposure effect happens even if you are not aware of this exposure. An important set of findings about the mere exposure effect is that even unconscious exposure increases the probability of positive appraisal—say, if the stimulus is flashed for a very short time (under 200 milliseconds) or if the stimulus is masked (that is, cleverly hidden). It is hard not to be slightly upset by these findings. We have some control over what kinds of music and art we are exposed to, but definitely not complete control. It is more and more difficult to be in any kind of public space without music. Cafés, shopping malls, elevators. The music you are exposed to in these places leaves its mark on your preferences and this is very rarely something we would be happy about.

Our aesthetic preferences in music, film, food, clothing, and art are super-important for us, and they can and do change in a way that we have no control over. If you are a fan of free jazz and you think of yourself as a free jazz person, being exposed to Justin Bieber's music in the supermarket will make you like the particular musical style of Justin Bieber's songs a little bit more. And you are very likely to have no idea about this. It happens under the radar.

If our preferences can be hijacked without us noticing, then a big part of who we are seems to be the product of random mere exposure. And we are defenceless against this. When I was young and pretentious, I made a point of always walking through the pop art rooms in museums with my eyes closed. But this is difficult (and a little bit dangerous) to pull off. And when it comes to music, even more difficult. Our taste changes and there is not much we can do about it. The mere fact that it is difficult not to

Aesthetics and the self

45

find this disconcerting shows just how important the aesthetic domain is for the self. But then we can't ignore this strong link between aesthetics and the self.

Experience versus judgement

Much of 'Western' aesthetics has been about well-informed aesthetic judgements. Aesthetic judgements are statements (often only to yourself, but sometimes also to others) that a particular object is beautiful or graceful or ugly or disgusting. But the vast majority of our aesthetic engagement is nothing like this. If it were, it would be difficult to explain why we care so much about all things aesthetic. The reason why we watch a three-hour-long film or take a day-long hike in the mountains is not to come up with a well-informed aesthetic judgement about the film or the landscape. If we take the importance of aesthetics in our life seriously, we need to shift the emphasis away from aesthetic judgements to forms of aesthetic engagement that are more enjoyable, more rewarding, and happen to us more often.

We do not go to a concert or cook for hours in order to pronounce aesthetic judgements. It is difficult to see why aesthetic judgements would matter for us that much. Making aesthetic judgements is really not that much fun, nor is it particularly rewarding. When we do take some kind of pleasure in making aesthetic judgements (say, when we rank our five favourite books or films, to post it on social media), this pleasure may have more to do with the communication of this judgement than with actually making the judgement. The same goes for long and intense debates with your friends about a film after seeing it in the cinema.

The temporal unfolding of our experiences in aesthetic contexts is, in contrast, fun, rewarding, and something we personally care about. It sometimes, but definitely not always, reaches its end point in an aesthetic judgement, but that is not why we are doing it. A major advantage of focusing on experiences and not on judgements is that it can help us understand the personal importance and urgency of all things aesthetic for the self.

But what is aesthetic judgement supposed to be? You go to the museum and look at a painting. You sit down in front of it and spend twenty minutes looking at it. Then you get up having formed an aesthetic judgement about it. And then you can communicate this aesthetic judgement to your friends or blog about it. Your experience of the painting lasts for twenty minutes. The judgement typically happens at the end of this process (although of course you can make judgements during the process, which you might revise later). 'Western' aesthetics has mainly focused on the judgement at the end of this process, not on the twenty-minute-long temporal unfolding of the experience (with its shifts of attention, visual comparisons, etc).

Aesthetic judgements don't even happen every time we engage with something aesthetically. It is an optional feature. Suppose that I spend twenty minutes in front of the painting but I just can't make up my mind about its aesthetic merits and demerits—I suspend judgement. This does not make my aesthetic engagement with the work of art any less rewarding or meaningful—or any less pleasurable. In fact, it can sometimes make your experience more pleasurable.

A lot has been said about how aesthetic judgements differ from other kinds of judgements. According to a broadly Kantian view, aesthetic judgement might not just be the end point of the experience; it might happen throughout and colour our experience itself. But even in this seemingly more experience-centred picture what matters most is the judgement. As long as we make the right judgement, it can lead us to have the right kind of experience. As we have seen extensively in Chapter 3, attention can change our experience radically. But aesthetic judgement very rarely can. Just because I believe that the picture is beautiful or graceful, my experience of it will be very unlikely to change (let alone change for the better). Attending to various thus far unnoticed features, in contrast, can change my experience significantly.

If we hold that aesthetics should be primarily concerned with the way our experience of the work of art unfolds temporally (whether or not this temporal unfolding culminates in an aesthetic judgement), then this general picture which begins with aesthetic judgements is just the wrong way of proceeding. We should not grant the assumption that we know the building blocks of all things aesthetic just because they are the building blocks of aesthetic judgements. We should examine our aesthetic engagement or experience in its own right and without borrowing any conceptual apparatus from the domain of aesthetic judgements.

Aesthetic experiences of our youth

Here is a striking demonstration of how the importance of aesthetics has little to do with our well-informed aesthetic judgement. Remember your very first strong aesthetic experience? As a child or maybe as a teenager? Some piece of music that just blew you away? A landscape that left you breathless? Here are three examples from my own life—feel free to change the examples to the ones from your youth.

Exhibit A: I was 16, standing in the old Tate Gallery (there was no Tate Modern then), mesmerized by a Clyfford Still painting. I must have spent two hours in front of it there and then. I didn't know much about Clyfford Still (1904–80) at that time. I knew he was an abstract expressionist, but that's about it. I loved the picture so much that the next day, when I was supposed to visit the Tower of London and the Houses of Parliament with my high school class, I left them, going back to Pimlico to have another look.

Exhibit B: rewind a year. I was so much into Michelangelo Antonioni's film *Blow-up* (1966) that I went to the cinema to see it two or three times a week. I knew the dialogues of the entire film by heart. Each time, I left the cinema in a state of rapture, of having understood something really important about love, appearance and reality, and other deep issues.

Exhibit C: rewind yet another year. I read a book that shook me to my core: Boris Vian's *L'Écume des jours* (1947). I had felt nothing like that ever before: I felt like laughing and crying at the same time.

The point I want to make is this: I now take *Blow-up* to be Antonioni's single worst film. *L'Écume des jours* is full of references I had no chance of understanding at age 14 and it's way less original than some of Vian's other novels. I still think that Clyfford Still is great, but there are also many other great works of art in that collection where, for some reason, I fell in love with this painting.

I went to Tate Modern just yesterday, in preparation for writing this chapter to see how I reacted. Well, not very strongly. I also watched *Blow-up* again (on my laptop, as cinemas don't seem to show Antonioni films any more), but I had to switch it off after twenty minutes or so, I just couldn't be bothered. And I put down the English translation of *L'Écume des jours* after a couple of pages (to be fair, it was because of the translation).

I had a much stronger and more rewarding aesthetic experience of these works of art when I first encountered them, knowing very little about art history, film history, or the history of 20th-century French literature than I do now, when I know a little more. I want to think that I am in a better position now to assess the aesthetic value of these works than I was at age 14–16. I can make a better aesthetic judgement now. But it is not as enthusiastic as it was then.

With my 20/20 hindsight, I should condemn the aesthetic judgement of the 14–16-year-old Bence, shouldn't I? But if I hadn't felt so strongly about these artworks, I would probably not have taken an interest in the arts and so wouldn't have picked up all the knowledge that now allows me to patronize the teenage Bence.

What would be a well-informed aesthetic judgement here? Take the judgement I just made about *Blow-up* being Antonioni's single worst film. That is the kind of judgement aesthetics should be about—we are told. The kind of liking I took in *Blow-up* as a 15-year-old is not what aesthetics is about.

My examples were intended to show that there can be, and there often is, a mismatch between the maturity of aesthetic judgements and the strength of our aesthetic experience. One conclusion that follows from this is that focusing exclusively on well-informed aesthetic judgements would leave something really important out of discussions of aesthetics: that aesthetic engagement is pleasurable and that it has some personal importance for us. We care about aesthetic engagement. An exclusive focus on well-informed aesthetic judgement cannot do justice to this very simple fact about aesthetics.

The primacy of experience

There is an even more important reason why I introduced these examples. We have seen that it is not the case that the better informed our aesthetic judgement is, the stronger or more rewarding our aesthetic experience gets. One consequence of this is that we should include strong, rewarding, and personally important aesthetic experiences in the discussion of aesthetics (and not sacrifice these for the exclusive focus on aesthetic judgements). But experiences are also prior to judgements in a very different sense. Each and every one of our well-informed aesthetic judgements relies on some earlier experiences that are rewarding, personally important to us, and not at all well informed.

When you step into a room with many paintings in a museum and take a quick look around, maybe you like some of the pictures on display, but not others. You have no idea who painted which picture, so any well-informed judgement is out of the question. But it is this initial liking that determines which painting you will approach and spend more time exploring. The only reason we are in the position to make all things considered well-informed aesthetic judgements is because we took a liking to some artworks earlier—maybe just seconds ago, or decades ago, and that's why we're engaging with this artwork and not some other one.

Let's take a step back. We have two instances of aesthetic engagement here. The experience I had as a teenager (very positive, very rewarding, very important for me personally) and the judgement I am making now (judging the work somewhat mediocre, not very rewarding, no importance for me personally). The latter is what we call a well-informed aesthetic judgement. And the latter could not have happened without the former. The question is this: what explains the aesthetic pleasure of the earlier aesthetic engagement? If we restrict our discussion to aesthetic judgements, it is difficult to see how we can answer this question. It can't be the maturity of our aesthetic judgement because the earlier aesthetic judgement was not at all mature or well informed. Maybe the strong and rewarding earlier experience was completely inadequate and aesthetically irrelevant, but then it would seem that inadequate and aesthetically irrelevant responses are largely responsible for our aesthetic preferences, as my current aesthetic preferences are very much a product of those aesthetic experiences of teenage Bence.

This is not a trivial problem. Here is one way of making it more urgent: why should I care about my well-informed aesthetic judgements if they leave me cold? They neither give me any pleasure nor are they of any personal importance to me. Why should we learn more about art history and the history of 20th-century French literature if the result is that we have less fun engaging with art?

Here is one way out of this conundrum. Aesthetic judgements are not that much fun. Neither the naive one of the kind I made as a teenager nor the well-informed one I am making now. Making judgements, in general, is rarely rewarding or entertaining or pleasurable. Experiences, on the other hand, can very much be rewarding or entertaining or pleasurable. Similarly, pronouncing judgements is rarely the kind of thing we find personally meaningful. Experiences are the kind of things we find personally meaningful. So aesthetics should be about experiences, not judgement. These experiences can lead to judgement, which we can communicate to others and that's a nice optional add-on, but they do not need to lead to judgement.

We spend so much time and money engaging with works of art not because we want to make aesthetic judgements about them. We do it because the experience we have while engaging with works of art can be pleasurable, rewarding, and personally meaningful. Not the judgement—the experience.

We should try to move away from the concept of aesthetic judgement in general—whether or not it is well informed. The aim of aesthetic engagement with an artwork is very rarely to come up with an aesthetic judgement and our aesthetic theory should respect this fact. We should focus on the temporal unfolding of our aesthetic experience and not on the (clearly optional) end point of pronouncing aesthetic judgements. As Susan Sontag said: 'A work of art encountered as a work of art is an experience, not a statement or an answer to a question.'

Why judgements?

In order to shift the emphasis of aesthetic theory from aesthetic judgement to the temporal unfolding of aesthetic engagement, we need to understand why aestheticians are obsessed with aesthetic judgements to begin with.

One reason is clearly historical. The key concept of 'Western' aesthetics has always been that of aesthetic judgement, at least since David Hume's 'Of the Standard of Taste' (1757)—which was published more than 250 years ago.

Hume (1711–76), whose influence on Anglo-American philosophical aesthetics is difficult to overstate, explicitly talks about the differences between the ways two different people make judgements of taste. He gives the following story as an illustration (borrowed from *Don Quixote*). Two people drink from the same wine and are asked to judge its quality. One of them says it has a discernible odd leathery taste. The other one thinks it has an unpleasant metallic note. The punchline of Hume's story is that while we might think that at least one of these judgements is just plain wrong, when the wine was inspected, they discovered a small key with a leather thong attached. So they were both right.

I will come back to this story in Chapter 5. But what matters for us now is that although Hume clearly stresses the importance of perceptual discrimination here, what he mainly cares about is the aesthetic judgement of these two wine connoisseurs. It does not matter for them how their experience of wine unfolded through time (although a lot can be said about how the experience of wine unfolds over time). The only thing that matters is the aesthetic judgement they came up with—and how the two judgements are related to one another.

As we shall see in Chapter 5, there are important philosophical reasons why Hume was focusing on judgements, but the strength of his influence on the field of aesthetics meant that his assumption that the central concern of aesthetics is understanding aesthetic judgements went unquestioned.

Another important historical reason for the dominance of judgements in aesthetics has to do with the strong influence of philosophy of language on philosophy in general and aesthetics in particular. Aesthetic judgements are statements (that we make to ourselves or to others) that philosophy of language has a lot to say about. So aesthetic judgement is a familiar subject for aestheticians with strong philosophy of language training. Experiences, in contrast, are not so easy to analyse using the conceptual toolkit of philosophy of language.

Going global

Here it is difficult not to point to the idiosyncrasy of this judgement-centred perspective if we broaden the scope of what we take to be aesthetics from strictly 'Western' aesthetics to global aesthetics. The vast majority of aesthetic traditions outside the 'West' are not too concerned with aesthetic judgements at all. They are concerned with the way our emotions unfold, the way our perception is altered, and the way aesthetic engagement interacts with social engagement.

The most extreme example comes from Islamic aesthetics (and especially Islamic aesthetics in the Sufi tradition). One way in which Islamic aesthetics is different from the aesthetic traditions of the 'West' is in its emphasis on the ever-changing nature of the world in general and of our experience of artworks in particular. And part of what is special about the engagement with art is our appreciation of these ever-changing, flickering experiences (an example would be the deliberately different views certain architectural features offer as we move around them, often further underlined by their fleeting reflections in water). This tradition is very much interested in beauty, but not with judgements about beauty, rather with the ways in which beauty could be explained in terms of the working of our perceptual system. And its emphasis on the ever-changing, flickering nature of our experience makes any attempt at a fixed judgement impossible.

We have also seen how Rasa theory is about the savouring of our multimodal emotional experiences, not judgements, which Rasa theory hardly talks about. On the rare occasion when what we would call aesthetic judgement is mentioned in Rasa theory, it is to show how stable and inflexible judgements would in fact work *against* this savouring of our experience. Finally, to give a somewhat obscure example, in Assyro-Babylonian aesthetics, the key concept of Tabritu is often translated as admiration and awe, but it is very clearly identified as the perceptual experience of the work, which involves 'repeated and continuous looking'—again, unfolding experience, not judgement. The fact that in our 'Western' tradition aesthetic judgement has played such an important role is little more than a historical curiosity.

A less historical, but more substantial reason why the concept of aesthetic judgement has dominated 'Western' aesthetics is that aesthetic judgements are communicable. When we have aesthetic disagreements, we have disagreements about aesthetic judgements: I say that the film was bad, you say it was good. So in order to understand the intersubjective and social aspects of our engagement with works, the argument would go, we need to focus on aesthetic judgements. The subject of Chapter 5 is this interpersonal dimension of aesthetics.

Chapter 5
Aesthetics and the other

Aesthetics is rarely a solitary endeavour. We share meals, we go to the museum with our friends, and we choose furniture for our flat together. When we go to a concert or to the cinema, we are in a room full of people who are having very similar experiences to ours. We are social beings and there are very few aesthetic situations that are devoid of all social aspects.

Further, it can be an important link between two friends if they have similar experiences when listening to the same song. And it can be alienating if your friend has a terrible experience while you have a mind-blowing one, while you both watch the same movie.

Aesthetic agreements and disagreements

It is somewhat unfortunate that the discussion of the social dimension of aesthetics in the history of 'Western' aesthetics has been dominated by one question and one question only: that of aesthetic agreements and disagreements.

Who is the better composer: Johnny Rotten or Wolfgang Amadeus Mozart? The intuition to be pumped here is that Mozart is the better one, everybody knows that. There is complete aesthetic agreement on this. And if there isn't, there should be. Those who prefer Johnny Rotten should know better. They should listen to more Mozart and then they will see the error of their ways.

In some sense the Johnny Rotten vs Mozart comparison is silly. There are probably very few heated late night arguments where one person (seriously) takes the side of Johnny Rotten and the other one defends Mozart. But we do very often argue about aesthetic matters—in fact, this is one of the most important things we argue about. Bach or Handel? Frida Kahlo or Diego Rivera? Or if these seem too highbrow, Beatles or Rolling Stones? *Seinfeld* or *Arrested Development*? Which *Fast & Furious* film? But also, to move away from art: is Han Solo or Luke Skywalker the more attractive? Is Paris prettier than Barcelona? Dark roast or light roast for coffee beans? Is steak better rare or medium rare? And so on.

Here are two obvious options for settling disagreements of this kind. We can agree to disagree. You like this, I like that. Neither of us is right, or, rather, we are both right. The other option is that one of us is just dead wrong. The plausibility of these two options will depend on which examples we pick. The Johnny Rotten vs Mozart case is a cheap shot at giving support to the second option. And the Frida Kahlo or Diego Rivera example could be seen as supporting the first one.

Compare aesthetic disagreements to disagreements about more prosaic things. If we both look at a painting, and I say it's square shaped, while you say it's triangle shaped, (at least) one of us is just mistaken. But if we look at the same painting and we disagree about its aesthetic qualities, things are less clear.

Another comparison would be with clearly 'subjective' disagreements. If we look at the same painting and I say it reminds me of my grandmother and you say it does not remind you of your grandmother, then these two opinions are consistent with each other (even if we have the same grandmother). I'm right and you are also right.

The question is whether aesthetic disagreement is closer to the 'square vs triangle' disagreement or to the 'reminds me of my grandmother or not' disagreement. And some of the central texts of 'Western' aesthetics tried to carve out an intermediate position between the purely 'subjective' disagreement (like the one involving my grandmother) and the purely 'objective' disagreement (like the one involving shapes).

Remember Hume's iron key with leather thong story? The reason why he gave this parable is exactly to tackle the problem of aesthetic agreements and disagreements. The two wine experts disagree. One discerns an iron taste, the other a leathery one. But it turns out that both are right. They are both right, but not because the judgement of taste is entirely 'subjective', but because there is an 'objective' basis for their judgement of taste: the key with the leather thong. But if a third expert had joined the party saying that the wine tastes of sulphur, she would be just mistaken. Judgements of taste are more restricted than judgements about what reminds me of my grandmother, but less restricted than judgements about shapes.

Aesthetics is not for policing

At this point of the aesthetic disagreement debate, one long and suspicious word invariably makes an appearance: normativity. The idea is that aesthetic evaluations have some kind of normative force. We *should* make certain kinds of judgement when appreciating certain objects. If we don't make these kinds of judgement, we err: we're not doing what we're supposed to be doing.

The general thought is that the domain of aesthetics is similar to the domain of morality in this respect: both are about what we should do and not about what we in fact do. Ethics tells us whether we should lie or steal or become vegetarians. And aesthetics tells us what kinds of aesthetic experiences we should have and when.

Normativity is about what we should do. And many aspects of our aesthetic life are very much normative in some respects. I myself have been making, and will continue to make, a fairly normative claim about how aesthetics should not privilege the 'West'. And it would be difficult to talk about some well-established aesthetic practices without making at least some normative claims about what, for example, performers of a musical piece *should* do for their performance to count as a performance *of* a certain musical piece (and not just of random notes). The word 'should' pops up all over the place when we talk about the aesthetic domain (and it pops up all over the place in this book as well).

Nonetheless, and I can't stress this strongly enough, aesthetics is not a normative discipline. Some parts of ethics might really be about normative claims (well, a branch of ethics is called 'normative ethics', so that would be a good candidate). But aesthetics is not. Aesthetics is not primarily about what we should do. It is about what we in fact do in what circumstances.

You might expect a work in ethics to convince you about whether you should become vegetarian or keep on eating meat. But you should not expect any works in aesthetics to give you that kind of advice. Aesthetics is not trying to tell you what you should do—which works of art you should admire and which ones to ignore. This way of thinking about aesthetics could go a long way towards dispelling the strong mistrust towards aesthetics as a discipline among many artists, who often feel that aesthetics is telling them what they are allowed to do and what they are not allowed to do and, more importantly, what kind of reaction is appropriate to their works.

Some branches of ethics might be about policing your behaviour in moral matters. But aesthetics is not about policing your aesthetic responses. Your aesthetic responses are what they are and you should not let anybody police them. As a result, we should view any appearance of words like normativity in aesthetics with great suspicion.

And this also goes for words like 'normativity' in the aesthetic disagreements debate. The general thought here is that aesthetic judgements or aesthetic evaluations have 'normative force'. This can mean many things. It can mean that your aesthetic reaction may be correct or incorrect. If you like works that are not to be liked, you're just wrong. If you dislike masterworks, you are wrong again. You *should* have a certain emotional or aesthetic reaction in the face of a certain work. If you don't, your aesthetic reaction is not what it should be. You are *wrong* to have this reaction.

If you don't like the authoritarian overtones of this line of thinking about the aesthetic, it is important to realize that this picture is deeply rooted in a very special (and very 'West'-centred) way of thinking about aesthetics. It is easy to see how we can make normative claims about aesthetic judgements. Judgements can be right or wrong and they are often wrong. But if we are interested in experiences, not judgements, then how could we even formulate normative claims? Here is an attempt. While experiences can't be right or wrong, they can be accurate or inaccurate. Perceptual illusions are inaccurate, for example. Just as you could misperceive the colour of an object, because it is too dark, you could also have an illusory aesthetic experience.

Crucially, this line of argument only works if we subscribe to what I labelled the beauty-salon approach to aesthetics: the view that what makes an experience aesthetic is that it is about beautiful things and that there is a hard division-line between beautiful things and non-beautiful things. When we have an inaccurate aesthetic experience, we experience a beautiful thing as non-beautiful (or a non-beautiful thing as beautiful).

But we have seen that the beauty-salon approach to aesthetics is not exactly an attractive view. What makes an experience aesthetic is not that it is about a beautiful thing. What makes it aesthetic is the way you exercise your attention. And there is no accurate or inaccurate way of exercising your attention. So while experiences may be accurate or illusory, what makes them aesthetic has nothing to do with their accuracy. It has everything to do with the way attention is exercised.

Let us go back to the aesthetic disagreements debate. The question there is about whether aesthetic disagreements are more like disagreements about the shape of the painting (you say triangle, I say square) or like disagreements about whether it reminds me of my grandmother. But even formulating this question takes for granted the beauty-salon approach to aesthetics.

If what matters for aesthetic engagement has little to do with the features attributed to the perceived object, then the comparison with disagreements about other attributed features, like shapes and whether it reminds me of my grandmother, are meaningless.

When you and I are looking at the same artwork or the same landscape, my experience might be very different from yours. But framing this difference as a disagreement either sneaks in an emphasis on aesthetic judgements (rather than experiences) or it commits us to the beauty-salon approach wholesale.

It matters for us if you and I have different experiences in front of the same artwork or landscape. It matters much more than a disagreement about shapes or about what reminds whom of their grandmother. And dumbing down the social dimension of aesthetic engagement to aesthetic disagreements fails to appreciate just how crucial aesthetics is in our everyday life and everyday social interactions.

Just one, somewhat embarrassing, example. The social dimension of aesthetics seems especially important in one's youth, when we tend to hang out with people who like the same music and despise others who like different music, for example. When I was in high school (and a huge snob, as we have seen in Chapter 4), I spent a summer in Germany allegedly learning German. I really liked one of the German girls and she really liked me and our budding relationship after various outings took us to her place. The first thing I remember seeing there was a giant Eros Ramazzotti poster, as she was a fan of this particular Italian pop singer.

There was a blatant aesthetic disagreement right there—let's just say that I was not one of Eros Ramazzotti's fans. But I powered through that little blip. It was when she dimmed the light and put on an Eros Ramazzotti CD in order to enhance the romantic mood that I just couldn't take it any more. Difference of opinion about aesthetic matters was OK. But when it came to being forced to have a shared romantic experience of Eros Ramazzotti's timbre, that was over the line.

Aesthetic disagreements matter, no doubt about that. But sharing or failing to share aesthetic experiences matters much more. And there are no right or wrong ways of having aesthetic experiences.

This does not mean that anything goes in aesthetics. Some artworks clearly try to evoke very specific reactions and if you have the opposite reaction, then something went astray. Suppose that you are sitting in front of your favourite painting in a museum. You are failing to have the experience you know that you could, and in some sense should, have in front of the painting in the museum. You are failing in an important sense, but this is not some kind of failing that needs to be policed.

As we have seen, we can change someone's aesthetic experience by drawing her attention to certain features. This is a much better way of dealing with differences of experience than cracking down on deviant ones. Lack of policing does not lead to anarchy. If we are lucky, it leads to conversation, peaceful coexistence, and diversity.

Back to normativity and its abuses. A more modest, but not at all less harmful, appeal to normativity, is about the universal appeal of aesthetic evaluations. It is not that a certain artwork just demands you to have a certain aesthetic reaction. Rather, when you have an aesthetic reaction, you implicitly assume that everybody else has, or at least should have, the same reaction. This is Immanuel Kant's view and it has had a lasting influence on 'Western' aesthetics.

I'm trying to say this politely and in awe of the intellectual achievement of Kant's philosophy, but this is one of the most arrogant ideas in the history of aesthetics. If you implicitly assume that everybody else should have the same reaction as you do, then you seriously underappreciate the diversity of humankind and the diversity of the cultural backgrounds people come from. And any time we are even tempted to think (or assume or feel) that whatever we do has universal appeal or universal communicability, that would be a good time to stop and exercise what I call 'aesthetic humility'—thinking about just how contingent our own position and cultural background is compared to the vast diversity of cultures on this planet. I will return to these themes in Chapter 7.

Aesthetic disagreements in real life

The real question about aesthetic agreements and disagreements is not about who is right and who is wrong. It is about the ways in which our experiences depend on the allocation of our attention, our background beliefs and knowledge as well as our past exposure. Knowing how these can alter our experience can help a lot in resolving aesthetic disagreements.

I used to work as a film critic. One of the better aspects of the job was to go to film festivals where I was often one of the jury members. Being on a jury at a film festival has its glamorous side—meeting famous actors and actresses, staying in fancy hotels, and so on. But it was also sometimes an exhausting and often infuriating experience.

You sit on a jury with four other people who are often from very different parts of the world and have very different taste in film from yours. But you need to come to some kind of decision about which film should get the prize. And there is always a strict deadline for doing so. You have to give the festival organizers a title by midnight. It's already 11 pm and there is no agreement about any of the films whatsoever. This is aesthetic disagreement in real life and resolving this disagreement is a task that Hume is not exactly helping with. After serving on juries a couple of times, the stale debates about aesthetic disagreement started to look very different to me.

What is going on in these jury meetings is not about sharing experiences, it is about hard aesthetic judgements. We had to agree that one film is better than the others. In fact, the way it actually worked was usually the other way round. First, we had to agree that some films would clearly not win the prize. This was the easier part. But then we were left with four or five remaining films and that's when the knives came out.

How do you try to convince another critic rationally that the film she liked was in fact derivative and clichéd? I'm afraid that the answer is that you don't and you can't. There was nothing rational about these debates. And, sadly, often the prize went to a film that none of the critics were crazy about, but that all of us could live with as the prizewinner.

The convincing was not rational—and I have seen very few critics trying to be rational. (Some more experienced critics were experimenting with some form of psychological warfare, systematically undermining, and sometimes unconsciously priming against, some films well before the jury discussion, and often during the screening. This psychological warfare was not rational either, but fought on a more emotional level. But I'm not sure much is to be learned from this for aesthetics in general other than the deviousness of critics...)

Almost the only thing that happened on these juries was trying to get other critics to attend to certain features of the films. This is not as obvious as it would be in the case of judging paintings or novels as film is a temporal art. We were days after having seen some of these films and what we could attend to was not the film itself, but rather our recollection of the film.

Nonetheless, almost all the arguments were really ways of directing the other critics' attention to some thus far unnoticed feature. Attending to this feature could make a negative aesthetic difference—when the aim was to dismiss this film. But it could also make a positive aesthetic difference—an argument for why this film is better than the rest of the field.

And this is in fact what critics should do, not only when they are on the jury, but also when they write reviews. This is what good critics actually do. Not treating criticism as an art form, as Pauline Kael (1919–2001), the iconic American film critic, did. Not summarizing the plot. Not telling their childhood memories very loosely connected to the plot. Not telling us what they liked and what they didn't. The critic's job is to direct our attention to features we would not have noticed otherwise. Attending to some of these features can completely transform our experience.

Some of these features may be structural—for example, how a theme on page 12 of the novel returns on page 134 and then again on page 432 and 563, and how this gives a structure to the otherwise unstructured narrative. Some others may be about links to other works of art—how a musical work quotes a tune from another musical work, for example. Attending to some of these features might make our experience more rewarding. And that makes reading critics actually worth the effort.

Here is a real-life example: a small painting from 15th-century Italy, depicting the Annunciation (Figure 4). The painter (Domenico Veneziano, c.1410–1461) had a little fun with the axes of symmetry: the symmetrical building is off-centre—it's pushed to the left of the middle of the picture. And the 'action' is also off-centre—but it is pushed to the right, not to the left. Attending to the interplay between these three axes of symmetry (of the building, of the picture itself, and of the axis halfway between Mary and the archangel) is not something everybody notices immediately. But when it is pointed out and your attention is drawn to it, this can make a huge aesthetic difference.

In terms of sheer quantity, there has never been as much criticism as there is today with literally hundreds of thousands of blogs and websites. But this just makes it even more obvious that criticism is in crisis. As Terry Eagleton (1943–), the British literary critic, eloquently put it more than thirty years ago (way before blogs), 'criticism today lacks all substantive social function. It is either part of the public relations branch of the literary industry, or a matter wholly internal to the academies.' One thing that has changed since then is the emergence of the celebrity critic who opines about films, music, and TV shows (often in front of live audiences) without doing much else. But the social function of criticism can be restored if critics just do what they are paid to do, namely, guide the reader's attention to features that could make an aesthetic difference.

André Malraux (1901–76), the French novelist, said that the primary aim of writing about art is not to enable the reader to

4. Domenico Veneziano, *Annunciation* (15th century), Fitzwilliam Museum, Cambridge.

understand art, but to persuade her to love it. Pontificating about art is of course much easier, but the critic is only doing her job if she helps the reader attend to the work in a way that persuades her to love it.

Aesthetic agreements in real life

Another important lesson I learned from being on the jury at film festivals was, oddly, not about aesthetic disagreements, but about aesthetic agreements. I found myself agreeing again and again with some critics in spite of the fact that they were from completely different continents and often they were fifty or so years my senior. And this made me wonder about what it is that explains this convergence between the aesthetic evaluations of a 20-something Hungarian living in the US and, say, a 70-something Argentinian living in Hong Kong.

And what I noticed more and more often is that these critics and I grew up watching very similar films. We liked the same films from the festival offering because we were primed to like them by the films we watched as teenagers. This was a hunch then, but as it turns out, there are some hard psychological findings that support this hunch.

As we have seen, the mere exposure effect is the well-known phenomenon that repeated previous exposure to a stimulus makes the positive appraisal of this stimulus more likely and this effect is also present in the aesthetic domain. But there is an important distinction to be made between two different kinds of mere exposure findings. The experiment I mentioned in Chapter 4 (about the Cornell professor showing slides with seemingly random impressionist paintings during class) was about how being exposed to one *specific painting* makes you like *that painting* more. But other mere exposure findings are about how input *of a certain kind* makes you like input *of that kind* more. So seeing many impressionist paintings could make you like another impressionist painting—one you have never seen before—more. And this means that the kind of artworks you have seen before deeply influence what kinds of artworks you will like.

If you watched 1960s black-and-white formalist French and Italian films in your formative years, then you will like films that resemble those in some broad manner (in their composition or maybe in their narrative). And this is true no matter whether you grew up in Budapest or in Buenos Aires.

The mere exposure effect may be even more salient in music: the kind of music you listened to in your formative years (which above all means early childhood and teenage exposure) will have a huge impact on what music you will be drawn to as an adult. Musical taste changes—it often changes radically. But that does not mean that your old favourites just get overwritten. They will always have an influence on what music you like.

In Chapter 4, I wrote about the worrying aspects of the mere exposure effect for just how unnoticeable the changes to our aesthetic preferences can be. But the mere exposure effect is not all bad. Knowing about how our aesthetic preferences are rooted in our very specific cultural and perceptual background can help us dial down our aesthetic arrogance and push us towards aesthetic humility.

Aesthetic humility

If you have listened to thrash metal since the age of 8, your aesthetic preferences are going to be very different from someone who grew up only listening to traditional Indonesian gamelan music. Nothing surprising so far. You will be sensitive to nuances that the gamelan fan will not even hear. You can attend to features in thrash metal that very few others will notice.

I will probably trust you and not my gamelan connoisseur friend if I want to figure out which Slayer album to listen to, because you will be a much more reliable source. But that is not the end of the story. The mere exposure to thrash metal will make you have aesthetic preferences for certain musical forms and rhythms that will probably colour your engagement with any other musical works.

Suppose I make both you and my gamelan friend listen to some early 20th-century Viennese atonal music or some seriously dissonant New York free jazz. You will both like some of these pieces and dislike others. But part of what makes you like this piece and not that one is your exposure to thrash metal. (I hope it is clear that I am not trying to dismiss thrash metal here—the same thing would happen if an atonally trained person listened to thrash metal for the first time.) And my gamelan-trained friend will like different pieces because of her mere exposure to gamelan music.

You might say that there is aesthetic disagreement here. But is there? What this example shows us is that we make aesthetic evaluations from the very specific perspective of our past exposure to certain works of art (and other stimuli). This does not mean that our past exposure fully determines our aesthetic evaluations. But it anchors these aesthetic evaluations and it will always show up in them. In this sense, all aesthetic evaluations are tied or indexed to the evaluator's cultural and perceptual background. Your evaluation of the atonal piece is tied to your thrash metal cultural background. My friend's evaluation of the very same piece is tied to her gamelan background.

It makes no sense to ask who is right and who is wrong. If aesthetic evaluations are indexed to the cultural background of the evaluator, then there is no actual aesthetic disagreement here, because you are making an evaluation indexed to a thrash metal cultural background and my gamelan friend is making an evaluation indexed to a very different cultural background.

This does not mean that there are no facts of the matter about aesthetic evaluation; it does not mean that anything goes when it comes to aesthetics. It just means that aesthetic evaluations are relative to the cultural background of the evaluators. If two evaluators have the very same cultural background and they disagree, this would indeed be a genuine aesthetic disagreement—one of them would be right and the other one wrong.

I made this thrash metal/atonal music example a bit extreme. Nobody listens to only one kind of music. Even if you are a huge thrash metal fan, you can't just filter out all other music (like that Justin Bieber at the mall). But this does not change the force of the argument that your aesthetic evaluations are a function of your cultural background. What follows from this is that you should be aware of your cultural background when making aesthetic evaluations. Your aesthetic evaluation is not some kind of universal standard. It is a very specific affair, deeply rooted in your very contingent cultural background. So we should treat all things aesthetic with a fair amount of humility.

Chapter 6
Aesthetics and life

Aesthetics is about special moments. But are these moments isolated islands in our otherwise dull daily routine? I don't think so. If you're lucky, you can have as many as three aesthetic experiences before breakfast.

But art as well as our engagements with all things aesthetic can also influence our life in a more prosaic manner. You dress like one of the characters in your favourite movie (probably without being aware of it), you use phrases you learn from sitcoms. And looking at photography helps people to see, as Berenice Abbot (1898–1991), the avant-garde photographer, says. Aesthetics and life are intertwined on all kinds of levels.

Life as a work of art?

The importance of the aesthetic for our life does not mean that we need to resort to cheap self-help slogans. One breathtakingly popular and influential such idea is that we should turn our life into—or treat our life as—a work of art. I want to make it clear how what I am saying is different from this.

Everyone who is anyone in 'Western' modernity endorsed some version of this metaphor, from Johann Wolfgang von Goethe (1749–1832) and Friedrich Nietzsche (1844–1900) to Marcel

Duchamp (1887–1968). So much so, that Robert Musil (1880–1942), the Austrian novelist, author of *The Man Without Qualities*, was having some fun stretching this line of self-help advice to its breaking point:

> What sort of life is it that one has to keep riddling with holes called 'holidays'? Would we punch holes in a painting because it demands too much from us in appreciation of the beautiful?

If you squint, you could see how this life as a work of art idea could make some kind of sense in the 19th century, when works of art were well-constructed coherent wholes. I can see someone striving to turn their life into a Jane Austen (1775–1817) novel, which has a beginning, a middle, and an end, in this order, and a nice coherent, and often moving, arc connecting these. But turning your life into a Marguerite Duras (1914–96) novel, where literally nothing happens, or a Roberto Bolaño (1953–2003) novel, where only terrible things happen, would be a very dubious enterprise.

The more general problem is that art has become too much like life. In fact, the big slogan of the art movements in the last half-century or so (at least since fluxus and pop art) has been that art should not be cut off from life. So if art becomes like life, then turning your life into a work of art either makes no sense or it is pure anachronism. There is even a sub-genre of visual art where the artist cuts actual holes into their pictures, which makes the Musil quote even funnier.

But maybe I'm not being charitable enough. Maybe the main idea here is not that our life should be turned into a work of art, but rather that our attitude towards life should be like our attitude towards a work of art.

This approach is not without its heroes either. Albert Camus (1913–60), in his largely forgotten novel *A Happy Death* (1938), writes that 'like all works of art, life also demands that we think about it'. A nice one-liner, but the reference to works of art is really a red herring. Lots of things demand that we think about them—philosophy books, news from the White House, the mystery of why Cinderella's shoe would fall off if it fitted her perfectly.

So works of art are not particularly helpful in this respect to compare life to. And while some works of art surely demand thinking about them, what kind of explicit thought would be appropriate as a response to the *Brandenburg Concertos* (1721) or a Mondrian painting? Camus's bon mot does not really add anything new to the old 'unexamined life not worth living' mantra.

Lots of things can be art. And there are lots of ways to relate to works of art, none of them are inherently better than others. So urging us to turn our life into a work of art—or to relate to life as if it were a work of art—is neither helpful nor particularly meaningful.

Spectators of our own life?

There is another popular way of connecting aesthetics and our life that I want to keep a safe distance from. In some ways it is a version of the treating your life as a work of art idea, but a very specific version. The gist is that the right attitude to have both towards life and towards works of art is to be detached spectators. As Oscar Wilde would put it, we should become the spectators of our own life.

This general idea was very influential in much of the 19th and 20th centuries. And many works of art created in the 'West' in the last couple of hundred years were clearly going for this effect. Many of the literary greats I cite in this book (from Pessoa to Proust) very clearly subscribe to this idea of aesthetic engagement. Even Susan Sontag, otherwise very discerning about sweeping claims concerning art, jumps on the bandwagon when she says that 'all great art induces contemplation, a dynamic contemplation'.

An advantage of taking the role of attention in aesthetic experience seriously is that we can explain why this kind of detached, contemplative experience has been a central metaphor but also how it is not a necessary feature of all aesthetic engagement. The kind of engagement Sontag, Proust, or Pessoa talk about can be characterized as open-ended attention roaming freely across the features of the artwork.

As we have seen, this way of exercising your attention accounts for a historically and geographically very specific form of aesthetic experience, which overlaps with the kind of experiences labelled as contemplation fairly well. But this is still just one kind of aesthetic experience, regardless of how influential it was in Europe in, say, the first half of the 20th century. Aesthetic experience does not have to be detached, it does not need to be contemplative, and it does not need to involve open-ended attention.

Many devotees of the idea of being spectators of our own life became very suspicious of this very concept in the light of the political events of the 1930s. The French novelist André Gide (1869–1951) wrote in his diary in 1934, a year after Hitler's rise to power, that 'whoever remains contemplative today demonstrates either an inhuman philosophy or monstrous blindness'.

More generally, the emphasis on contemplation seems to go against the undeniable political elements in art. Contemplation is often seen as apolitical, and choosing contemplation instead of political activity, in troubled times, is often regarded with suspicion.

And regardless of how we think about aesthetics, we should not automatically remove politics from the domain of aesthetics, nor should we remove aesthetics from the domain of politics. The emphasis on contemplation leads easily to some kind of sharp opposition of politics and aesthetics, but any such opposition would just be historically and psychologically inaccurate.

To the contrary, aesthetic actions have been, and still are, an important vehicle of political ideas. In fact, this is an important aspect of the social relevance of aesthetics. One of the most memorable aesthetic experiences of my youth was a demonstration against the Russian occupation of Hungary in 1988, when completely unexpectedly we could freely chant 'Russians go home' in a large crowd without having to fear a police crack-down. I really like Stendhal's take on this connection (which also emphasizes the concept of attention): 'in literary works politics is like a gunshot during a concert. It is a bit vulgar, but it does make everybody pay attention immediately.'

How about the contemplation of your own life? The idea that a good life means having a contemplative relation to our life goes hand in hand with the emphasis on contemplative aesthetic experiences. And it is easy to see how this is a line some more current self-help schools like the Stoic/Buddhist revival or mindfulness would exploit with a vengeance. We have seen that contemporary art has moved away from contemplation. And it is the diminishing role of contemplation in our artworld that made it so easy for the mindfulness industry to take over that niche.

The link between life and aesthetics is way more important and rewarding than just a platitude about contemplation. Aesthetic experiences can help us avoid being jaded. They can teach us new ways of seeing the world.

How not to be jaded

I talked about the philosophical lessons that being a film critic taught me. But being a film critic also has a pretty depressing side.

You have to spend a lot of time with other film critics, many of whom have been in the job for many decades.

Maybe I was unlucky, but I had to spend a lot of time with film critics who were incredibly jaded. They said (often and loudly) how much they loved film, but I saw very little trace of this. They complained about every single film we watched together, and even the ones they did not absolutely hate they only saw through the angle of what they could say about them at the prize deliberations or in their review.

The reason I gave up being a film critic and decided to live the much less glamorous life of an academic is that I didn't want to be like them. I did not want to become jaded. I did not want to forget how to be truly touched and moved and lifted by a film or by other works of art.

But what did these people do wrong? How did they become so jaded? Take one example: Ronnie (which may or may not be his real name). Ronnie was English—very English. He wrote for one of the top British newspapers, but he also had side-gigs in pretty much all of the quality print media of the United Kingdom. He was not young. He had spent his youth in Paris, hobnobbing in the literary and film scene of the 1960s with the likes of Jeanne Moreau and Jean-Luc Godard. This is what he rooted his entire identity as film critic in: he was there at this vibrant and exciting period of film history, getting drunk with actors on the sets of films that now count as classics.

Ronnie and I became very good friends in spite of our age difference partly because our tastes in art and film converged to a surprising degree. But Ronnie measured every contemporary film to his beloved classics, which is not a particularly helpful attitude if you spend half of your life on the festival circuit, where your job is to watch contemporary films. And Ronnie's attitude was not at all unusual among film critics: I have seen a lot of cultural pessimism and the glorification of the past in these circles. If these critics could get their kicks out of watching old films, but not new ones, then they may have been wasting their time on the festival circuit. But maybe they were not jaded at all. They just watched the wrong films. Or so I thought initially.

One night at the Chicago International Film Festival, after a particularly difficult jury decision and a lot of Amaretto, Ronnie confessed that he no longer got any pleasure out of seeing his old favourites. He said that sometimes he understood some interesting connections to other films or noticed some nuance that he could then write about in some review or article. But he no longer felt anything. Ronnie, understandably, was pretty cut up about this. And so was I.

Since then I've realized that this is a fairly widespread phenomenon among professional art critics and even art historians. Ernst Gombrich (1909–2001), probably the most widely known art historian of the 20th century, was in the exact same predicament. He could give a nuanced artistic and historical analysis of pretty much any painting he looked at, but the whole experience left him completely cold.

In fact, I was beginning to notice the signs of this in myself, with horror. I enjoyed watching films less and less, especially when I knew I had to write a review about them. And I have to admit that Ronnie was absolutely remarkable in that after seeing a film, he could just sit down and write a first-rate, sophisticated, and knowledgeable two-page review about it in ten minutes. So, I thought, maybe the price to pay for becoming a truly professional film critic is that we have to stop enjoying films? This possibility terrified me. Maybe this whole enjoyment-of-art thing is for amateurs only? True professionals don't waste time on that?

I don't think I have a good answer to these questions. But my stint as film critic did teach me to see what it was that Ronnie and his colleagues (and also, at least for some time, even myself) were doing: they had very clear and fixed expectations about what they were going to see when they sat down in the movie theatre.

Sweet, and not so sweet, expectations

Expectation is a good thing. Without having expectations about what is around us, we could do very little. And expectations also play a crucial role in our engagement with art: when we are listening to a song, even when we hear it for the first time, we have some expectations of how it will continue. And when it is a tune we know, this expectation can be quite strong (and easy to study experimentally). When we hear Ta-Ta-Ta at the beginning of Beethoven's *Fifth Symphony* (1808), we will strongly anticipate the closing Taaam of the Ta-Ta-Ta-Taaaam.

There is a lot of scientific research on how expectations can influence our experience—of music, of pain, of everything. And many of our expectations are fairly indeterminate: when we are listening to a musical piece we have never heard before, we will still have some expectations of how a tune will continue, but we don't know what exactly will happen. We can rule out that the violin glissando will continue with the sounds of a beeping alarm clock (unless it's a really avant-garde piece), but we can't predict with great certainty how exactly it will continue. Our expectations are malleable and dynamic: they change as we listen to the piece.

My suspicion is that the jaded critics' expectations are not so malleable and dynamic. Ronnie knew exactly what he could expect when the lights went off. No doubt, sometimes the film surprised him, but even if it did, it surprised him in a predictable manner: 'Aha, so the director chose a narrative twist that is reminiscent of Hitchcock, not of film noir!' The space of possibilities of what the film could do was already mapped out in his head at the very beginning. And the only degree of uncertainty was which of the already very clearly defined and understood rubrics the film would end up in.

Of course, the more you know about film, the more patterns of comparisons you will have, and it is very difficult to do anything in film that has not been done before. If you know the entirety of film history inside out, it is difficult to ignore these potential parallels, contrasts, and comparisons. But this can make your experience a mere classification job: the storyline was like *Indiana Jones* (1981), the composition like *Avatar* (2008), the acting like *Napoleon Dynamite* (2004). There's not much fun in watching films that way.

What is missing is some degree of openness and willingness to let yourself be genuinely surprised. Not just surprised about which carefully delineated film-historical pigeonhole the film ends up in. But surprised about what the film does to you.

The jaded film critic's attention is very much focused. Ronnie will focus on a couple of clearly defined features that he thinks will be relevant for his review. And he will ignore all the rest. And often rightly so, because the rest will probably be pretty predictable. But sometimes it will not be. And Ronnie will miss out on anything that happens outside the focus of his attention.

But if we watch a film with less clearly defined expectations (or should I say preconceptions?), we will not immediately discount everything that is outside the scope of those features we think are relevant. Everything can be relevant, even those things that the professional critic considers to be a waste of time.

André Breton (1896–1966), poet, artist, and the doyen of the Parisian Surrealist movement in the 1920s and 1930s, did not like cinema so much. He found it too predictable and too real—not quite up to his Surrealist standards. But he found a way to enjoy cinema by putting his opened-up left hand in front of his eyes, so he could not see the entire screen, only slices of it. And he claimed to have great experiences that way. Not something Ronnie would do, and, frankly, not something I would recommend to any budding film critic, but clearly a more enjoyable experience than Ronnie's.

By covering up half the screen, André Breton managed to get rid of his preconceptions of what would happen, and he could have a truly open experience of what was on the screen. Again, this is an extreme example, which would clearly not work for everyone. (And just imagine the sight of the entire audience covering up their eyes—not every film director's dream.) But that was André Breton's way of fighting the tendency to become jaded. What he did was to force his attention not to look for the usual stereotypical things one attends to. He forced his attention to be open and unconstrained by expectations. And there must be ways of doing this without covering your eyes.

Seeing afresh

About the same time that Breton was watching films through his fingers, the Italian painter Giorgio de Chirico (1888–1978) was painting hauntingly beautiful but also somewhat disconcerting paintings, with empty piazzas, arches, ancient sculptures, and trains in the distance. He had a particular talent for transforming everyday scenes into something out of this world. And he also had a lot to say about this:

> One clear autumnal afternoon I was sitting on a bench in the middle of the Piazza Santa Croce in Florence. It was of course not the first time I had seen this square. [...] The whole world, down to the marble of the buildings and the fountains, seemed to me to be convalescent. In the middle of the square rises a statue of Dante draped in a long cloak, holding his works clasped against his body, his laurel-crowned head bent thoughtfully earthward. The statue is in white marble, but time has given it a gray cast, very agreeable to

the eye. The autumn sun, warm and unloving, lit the statue and the church façade. Then I had the strange impression that I was looking at all these things for the first time.

What I find the most spot-on about this quote is the last sentence. When we have strong experiences in front of an artwork or landscapes, we often see it as if we were looking at it for the first time. In fact, a good way of characterizing at least some forms of aesthetic experience is that it feels as if it is the very first time we are having this experience. Even if we have seen it many times before, when it really touches us, it feels like it's the first time. We've never *really* seen it before. But now we do.

This 'seeing it for the first time' line may sound like a corny cliché. I think it's more than that. When you see something for the first time, you have no established and routine way of looking at it—of singling out those features that are relevant to you and of ignoring the rest. You move your attention around, as any of its features could be relevant. So when you see something for the first time, your attention tends to be open-ended—you have no clear idea what to focus on.

If you suddenly have to put out a fire in your friend's apartment and you see an object (even an artwork) for the first time, you probably won't move your attention around in search of rewarding features. You'll just look out for one and only one thing: how it can help you with putting out the fire. But if you are not in a hurry to do anything in particular and you are interested in an object you've never seen (and that's what happens in the museum, typically), your attention tends to be open-ended. The feeling that you're looking at something for the first time is an indication that your attention is open-ended.

When you feel that you're looking at something for the first time, this means that you've left behind any established and routine way of looking at it. And this is the contrast I am interested in: routine and habitual ways of looking at something and the 'as if for the first time' way of looking at it. This is what De Chirico was talking about: his routine and habitual way of relating to the world just stopped suddenly and he saw the world afresh.

Of course, there is nothing wrong with the routine and habitual. When driving to work, navigating a traffic jam, it is great to have the routine and habitual way of perceiving: in these occasions, you don't want to look at things afresh. Also, seeing afresh is difficult to maintain for more than just a couple of minutes. You can't be in this aesthetic trance 24/7.

Remember that song that you listened to over and over again as a teenager? Blew you away each time. Until, well, it just stopped blowing you away. It's as if you used it up; you got too used to it. Whenever that happened to me, I had a real feeling of loss.

The good thing is that at least sometimes this experience can come back. You stop listening to the song for a while and when, a couple of months (or years) later, you hear it again, it might blow you away even more strongly than ever before. And then, it *is* as if you were listening to it for the first time. The habits and routines melt away.

This was the key insight of De Chirico and his Parisian friends a hundred years ago: art can help us to overcome the habits and routines of our prosaic everyday perception. Habits grind you down. Even the most beautiful things will look paler and paler the more you look at them. But art can help you to let your habits go, and to look at something in a way you never have.

This 'seeing afresh' feeling obviously does not capture all we care about in aesthetic experiences. As we have seen, not all aesthetic experiences are characterized by the kind of open-ended attention that is at play when you see things as if you saw them for the first time. We clearly cherish listening to the same song hundreds of times, watching the same movie until we know all the lines by heart, and so on. And we do enjoy the feeling of familiarity when we do so. Marcel Duchamp called art 'a habit-forming drug', no less. Aesthetic experiences come in different flavours. But some aesthetic experiences have a lot to do with seeing something as if we saw it for the first time.

The lingering effect

Here is another way in which the aesthetic colours our life. Aesthetic experiences can have a lingering effect. This is one odd and underexplored aspect of enjoying art: that it lingers. When you spend an entire day in the museum and you walk home afterwards, the drab bus stop may look to you like one of the pictures in the museum. And when you're leaving a good concert or movie, the ugly, grey, dirty streetscape can look positively beautiful.

Marcel Proust describes the same phenomenon. After seeing his favourite painter's work (he uses the fictional name of Elster to refer to him), he began paying attention to features in the prosaic dining room scene that he had never paid attention to before. He saw this scene that he had seen many, many times before very differently. Suddenly, he began to attend to

> the broken gestures of the knives still lying across one another, the swollen convexity of a discarded napkin upon which the sun would patch a scrap of yellow velvet, the half-empty glass which thus showed to greater advantage the noble sweep of its curved sides, and, in the heart of its translucent crystal, clear as frozen daylight, a dreg of wine, dusky but sparkling with reflected lights, the displacement of solid objects, the transmutation of liquids by the effect of light and shade, the shifting colour of the plums which passed from green to blue and from blue to golden yellow in the half-plundered dish, the chairs, like a group of old ladies, that came twice daily to take their places round the white cloth spread on the

table as on an altar at which were celebrated the rites of the palate, where in the hollows of oyster-shells a few drops of lustral water had gathered as in tiny holy water stoups of stone…

As he says, 'I tried to find beauty there where I had never imagined before that it could exist, in the most ordinary things, in the profundities of "still life".'

One of the advantages of emphasizing the importance of attention in aesthetic engagement is that it can explain this puzzling phenomenon. Art changes the way you attend. And this attentional state of mind doesn't stop just like that. It lingers on.

Aesthetic experiences can make us ditch our preconceived way of making sense of what we see. When we're done with the art, our attentional freedom takes some time to change back. We keep on approaching whatever we see with open-ended attention. And this can lead to seeing the dirty sidewalk in front of the cinema as a work of art.

Ad Reinhardt (1913–67), the American abstract painter, says that 'looking isn't so simple as it looks. Art teaches people how to see.' And this is one important perk we get from enjoying art: it can make you recover the uncomplicated pleasure of seeing—regardless of what it is that you are seeing. It *can* make you see things as if you were looking at them for the very first time.

Chapter 7
Global aesthetics

Think back to your last visit to a major art museum. Can you recall how many of the 'must see' artworks in the museum were made in Europe or the US? Probably the vast majority of them. But artworks have been made in all parts of the world, not only in Europe and the US. These artworks are not easy to spot in most art museums. If they are there at all, they tend to be tucked away in some distant wing.

Willem de Kooning (1904–97), the abstract expressionist painter, compared the dominant contemporary vision of art history to a railway track: 'There is a train track in the history of art that goes back to Mesopotamia. It skips the whole Orient, the Mayas, and American Indians. Duchamp is on it. Cézanne is on it. Picasso and the Cubists are on it; Giacometti, Mondrian, and so many, many more—whole civilizations.'

Luckily, few art historians subscribe to this single railway track vision of art history these days. But this way of thinking about art still dominates everyday conceptions of art and also curatorial work in most museums. If we want to stop privileging European art over any other kind of art, we need to change not just the imbalance between 'Western' and non-'Western' art, but also the imbalance between 'Western' and non-'Western' aesthetics. We need a global aesthetics.

The geography of vision

How does your aesthetic experience (your experience of artworks, landscape, etc.) depend on what culture you grew up in? This is the starting question of global aesthetics. And the answer is straightforward: we can't just assume that artefacts are perceived everywhere and in every historical era the way they are perceived here and now. (I will talk about artefacts from now on because I want to stay away from the question about what does and what does not count as 'art' in which cultures.)

This claim goes against a traditional view in aesthetics, according to which aesthetics as a discipline is about universals: it examines ways of engaging with artworks and other aesthetic objects that are independent of our cultural background. In fact, art historians often accuse aestheticians of this kind of cultural universalism. And this universalism of aesthetics is even more heavily emphasized by the recently fashionable neuroscientifically tainted aesthetic research, which often aims to find the neural correlates of various forms of aesthetic appreciation in a way that does not depend on the cultural background of the subjects.

In fact, it's the other way around. If we take the empirical sciences of the mind seriously, what they actually teach us is to abandon cultural universalism altogether. The reason for this is the well-documented abundance of top–down influences on perception. Thousands of studies in psychology and neuroscience demonstrate that what we know and believe influences even the earliest stages of visual and auditory processing. And given that we know and believe different things depending on what culture and what time period we grew up in, our perception will also be different depending on what culture and what time period we grew up in.

The question is how these top–down influences on perception work and what processes mediate them. I will talk about two such mediating mechanisms, attention and mental imagery. Both attention and mental imagery depend heavily on our higher order mental states, such as beliefs and knowledge. And both attention and mental imagery influence our perception and our aesthetic engagement.

To put it differently, there are cross-cultural variations in attention and mental imagery. And given the importance of attention and mental imagery in our aesthetic engagement, this guarantees that there will be cross-cultural variations in our aesthetic engagement. Knowing what we know about how the mind works, universalism is not an option. We can't assume that our engagement is the same as the engagement intended and practised by the local producers and users of the artefact.

What we are attending to and how we do so very much depend on our background beliefs, knowledge, and perceptual skills, all of which are culturally specific. So our patterns of attention are also culturally specific. But given that our experience of artefacts depends heavily on what we are attending to, this means that there is significant cross-cultural variation in our experience of artefacts.

Here is an example: look at the tepatu (breastplate) from the Solomon Islands shown in Figure 5. You probably see an abstract pattern of intersecting lines. Now I tell you that the inverted V shape at the lower end of the tepatu is likely to represent the tail of the frigate bird, and the shapes just above them are its wings. The frigate bird indicates the presence of schools of bonito, a fish crucial in the diet of inhabitants of Santa Cruz Islands, where this tepatu is from. The shapes further up are thought to represent dolphins or fish, maybe even the bonito that frigate birds signal.

You are likely to attend to different features of this tepatu before and after reading the previous paragraph. You pay more attention to parts of it that you ignored before (e.g. the little bumps which

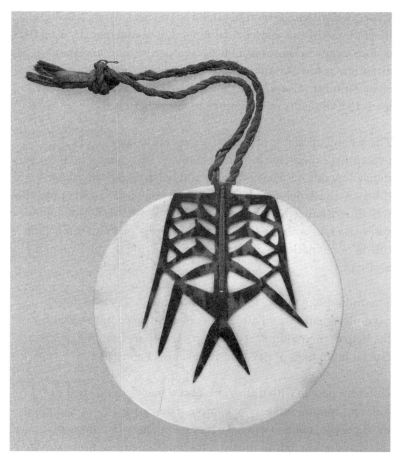

5. **Tepatu (or tema or tambe), Solomon Islands, late 19th century (Oceania), Metropolitan Museum of Art.**

may indicate the backs of dolphins). And, as a result, your experience is very different. Change in (very culturally specific) attention leads to change in your experience of the artefact.

And it is not just what we attend to that differs across cultures, but also the way we attend. People who grew up in East Asia tend to respond differently from Europeans to simple visual displays, like an aquarium. Europeans tend to attend to the moving fish, whereas East Asians tend to attend to the background features, like bubbles or the seaweed. In general, it seems that the attention of Europeans in these visual tasks is more focused and the attention of East Asians is more distributed. Again, there are cross-cultural variations in the exercise of attention, which then leads to cross-cultural variations in our experience.

The second mediator of the top–down influences on our perceptual experience is mental imagery. Our mental imagery very much depends on what we know and believe and what other things we have perceived before. When you visualize an apple, the way this visualized apple looks depends on what kinds of apples you've seen in your life. And mental imagery plays an important role in our experience of artworks (a recurring theme in Japanese aesthetics).

The Indonesian artist, Jompet Kuswidananto (1976–), for example, creates installations that need to be completed with the help of mental imagery. The spectator's mental imagery is a crucial ingredient of the experience here (Figure 6).

Different people with different cultural backgrounds will use different mental imagery to complete this artwork—presumably most people (not all) will have mental imagery of horses looking at this installation, but in those cultures where horses are associated with warfare, for example, this mental imagery (especially of the rider) will be very different and it will carry very different emotional charge. And this means that different people with different cultural background will have very different experiences of the very same artwork.

The Kuswidananto installation has unusually direct and explicit appeal on our mental imagery, but mental imagery is involved in almost all experiences of artworks. This is especially clear in almost all non-'Western' aesthetic traditions, where aesthetic experience is very explicitly taken to be a multimodal experience

6. Jompet Kuswidananto, *Cortège of the Third Realm*, 2012 (Indonesia).

that talks to all our sense modalities, not just to vision, but also hearing, smelling, tasting, and touching (the often quite extreme visuo-centrism of aesthetics seems to be a 'Western' thing).

This is most explicitly articulated in the Rasa tradition, where, as we have seen, Rasa literally means the savouring of the emotional flavour of experience. And flavour here is not a mere metaphor. Even those Rasa experiences that are triggered by only one sense modality (say, hearing, in the case of music) are supposed to exercise all of our other sense modalities (seeing, smelling, touching, tasting). In other words, they are supposed to evoke multimodal mental imagery.

And the Rasa is not an isolated example. A key concept in Japanese aesthetics is that of 'hidden beauty' or Yugen, the appreciation of which involves something akin to mental imagery (of the hidden and incomplete aspects). And the 11th-century Islamic philosopher Avicenna also heavily emphasized the importance of imagery in our experience of beauty.

Our experience depends on our cultural background. Art historians like to talk about the history of vision. Heinrich Wölfflin (1864–1945), probably the most influential art historian of all time, famously claimed that 'vision itself has its history, and the revelation of these visual strata must be regarded as the primary task of art history'. While a lot has been said about this provocative statement, there is one sense in which this claim is just empirically true: given that attention and mental imagery have a history, vision, which is influenced by these, also has a history.

If vision has a history in this sense, then vision also has a geography. And the same is true of perception in general. Given that attention and mental imagery are exercised depending on what culture we have grown up in, perception, which is influenced by these, also depends on our cultural background. Global aesthetics is about the geography of vision.

A global vocabulary

We can't use our own experience of an artefact to make assumptions about how this artefact is experienced in different cultures. But then how are we supposed to find out about how it is experienced and used in different cultures (especially if nobody is left from these cultures to talk to)?

We know a lot about some centres of artefact production. We know much less about others. This introduces a significant asymmetry into thinking about global aesthetics. We have a fair amount of information about how paintings were made and how people looked at them in 15th-century Italy and we know almost nothing about this in 15th-century Central America. This epistemic asymmetry is a result of coincidental factors like where records survived and where they did not. This should not lead us to think that artefacts in those parts of the world that we know more about are somehow 'better' or more worthy of study.

But if we can't extrapolate our 'Western' experience to other cultures and if we have very little information about how artefacts were experienced in most parts of the world, then this leads to a sceptical conclusion—we just have no way of knowing how other cultures experience artefacts because of the radical differences of the experience of artefacts in different cultures. If we want to avoid this sceptical conclusion, we need to find a way of understanding at least some aspects of artefacts without knowing much about the culture that produced them.

Global aesthetics must be able to have a conceptual framework that can talk about any artefact, no matter where and when it was made. This amounts to identifying features that every artefact needs to have and that are aesthetically relevant.

Some trivial examples of features that every artefact needs to have include material composition and size. Every artefact is made of something and every artefact is either this or that big. There are even more trivial features such as whether or not the artefact depicts an apple. It either does or it doesn't—there are no other options. The problem with these examples is that while in some cultures size and material composition may be aesthetically relevant, in many cultures, they are not. We need to find some feature-space that is more aesthetically relevant.

I want to use pictures as a case study. The experience of pictures can often be an aesthetic experience, and this is true not just in our 'Western' culture. Pictures are not necessarily artworks—for example, airplane safety charts about how to leave the plane in case of a water landing are not artworks by any account. Lots of things count as pictures: not just oil on canvas or tempera on wood, but also tattoos on one's skin, scratches on a piece of tree bark, or selfies on your phone. Pictures are a diverse bunch.

Nonetheless, every picture has pictorial organization: every picture organizes the pictorial elements in a non-random manner. And pictorial organization is aesthetically significant in all cultures. One of the key concepts of Yoruba aesthetics (the aesthetic tradition of the people of South-West Nigeria) is that of 'ifarahon', which is often translated as visibility—as the requirement that all parts of the person are clearly formed and visible. While this concept initially applied to sculptures, it has also become the most important virtue photographers should aim for (where it would, for example, imply that both of the sitter's eyes should be visible).

In the most detailed early work of Chinese aesthetics of painting, the 6th-century Chinese painter and critic Xie He outlined the six laws of painting. The fifth one is about placing and arranging on the surface the pictorial elements in space and depth (which became a central topic in all Chinese treatises on paintings from then on). The third Khanda of *Vishnudharmottara Purana*, the extremely detailed encyclopedic Hindu text on painting, written about the same time, is also full of references to pictorial organization—who should be behind or next to or in front of whom. And pictorial organization has been a central topic of Japanese aesthetics as well.

The question all these works ask is how pictures are organized. On a very abstract level, there are two different and distinctive modes of pictorial organization, which I call 'surface organization' and 'scene organization'. Every picture, regardless of where and when it was made, falls somewhere on the spectrum between surface organization and scene organization.

Surface organization aims to draw attention to how the two-dimensional outline shapes of the depicted objects are placed within the two-dimensional frame. Scene organization, in contrast, aims to draw attention to how the three-dimensional depicted objects are placed in the depicted space. There is a trade-off between the two and most pictures are trying to combine them. But one—either scene or surface organization—tends to win out when the two organizational principles are in conflict.

Pictorial organization is aesthetically relevant and all picture makers need to choose how to organize their pictures. And, crucially, this is not a 'West'-centric distinction—it is a design problem for pictures in any culture. Thus, the spectrum between scene organization and surface organization could be taken to be a starting point of a very general (but not 'West'-centric) conceptual framework for describing any pictures, regardless of where they were made.

The distinction between scene organization and surface organization is somewhat abstract. So it would be helpful to substantiate this distinction with the help of simpler features that are easier to spot. I will focus on two such features: occlusion and empty surface.

In everyday perception, we get a lot of occlusion: we see some objects behind or in front of other objects. The question is whether occlusion shows up in pictures. Surface organization implies that the picture maker pays attention to whether there is occlusion or not: occlusion in a picture is a feature of how two-dimensional outline shapes of the depicted objects are related to each other on the two-dimensional surface. Some pictures go out of their way to avoid occlusion. Some others pile on occlusions. Both are good indications of surface organization. And we can place all pictures on a spectrum between extreme lack of occlusion and extreme seeking out of occlusion. Figures 7 and 8 are two examples that are close to the two end points.

Pictures from some cultures will cluster around specific points of this occlusion spectrum. The Scythian pictures of Pazyryk, for example, tend to avoid occlusion at almost all costs. In Hanegawa

7. **Scythian wall-hanging, 5th century BCE, Pazyryk, Altai (Siberia).**

Toei's image, almost everything seems to be deliberately occluded. Both of these types of pictures would count as having surface organization.

Pictures of some other cultures (for example, Plane Native American carvings or Dutch still life paintings from the 17th century), in contrast, are not particularly bothered by the presence or lack of occlusion—this is an indication of scene organization: if a picture is organized in terms of the three-dimensional scene it depicts, then neither occlusion nor the lack of occlusion will be particularly important.

The second feature that every picture has is the presence or absence of empty surface. In everyday perception, some of our visual field is often empty in the sense that there are no perceptually interesting elements there—only the sky, the ground,

8. Hanegawa Toei, *Procession of Korean Mission in Edo, c.*1748 (**Japan**).

an empty wall. Some pictures deliberately try to avoid empty surface: they try to put pictorially interesting elements on every square inch of the surface. Others deliberately seek out empty surfaces. Some examples are found in Figures 9 and 10.

Again, paying attention to whether some part of the surface is empty or not is very much an indicator of surface organization. Scene organization is neutral about whether some parts of the surface remain unfilled. As in the case of occlusion, pictures with surface organization will cluster around some specific points of the empty surface spectrum (pictures from different cultures around different points). Pictures with scene organization, in contrast, are scattered around much of this spectrum.

We get a coordinate system on the basis of these two features: occlusion and empty surface. And we can add other features like frame or symmetry. Some pictures respect or even emphasize their

9. Alexander Apóstol, Residente Pulido, 2001 (the photographer digitally removed many of the details (windows, doors) from the building) (Venezuela).

frame, others deliberately try to pretend that the frame is not there. And as the frame is very much a two-dimensional surface feature, paying attention to it (either by emphasizing it or by de-emphasizing it) is a sign of surface organization. Symmetry is another surface feature: going out of your way to get symmetrical

10. **Mural in Wat Pho, 19th century, Bangkok School (Thailand).**

compositions or going out of your way to get asymmetrical compositions would then be an indication of surface organization. If symmetry is not a big deal (or if the frame is not a big deal), that would be a sign of scene organization.

This gives rise to a multi-dimensional feature space where we can place every picture, regardless of how much we know about the culture that produced it. This is obviously not the end of our understanding of pictures from different cultures: there are so many other aspects of pictures that are culturally specific that this formal analysis will not be able to provide. But it is a solid starting point for any further, more culturally specific enquiry.

This culture-neutral multi-dimensional feature-space can help us to make some progress in understanding pictures of cultures we otherwise know very little about. If all pictures produced in a specific culture painstakingly avoid occlusion, for example, this gives us an important data point to try to find out why they do so. This formal analysis will not give us answers (or it may give us very partial answers), but it can make the questions we ask more focused.

Here is an example. If you knew nothing about medieval European culture and you saw many images like Domenico Veneziano's small painting we encountered in Chapter 5 (Figure 4), you would have no idea who the two figures in these images are. One of them is a woman, the other one has wings. But if you see enough images of this woman plus winged human pattern, you would notice that the two figures tend to be placed far away from each other. Not only do they not occlude one another, but they are placed on the canvas in such a way that they could not possibly occlude one another. You do not know that these are images of the Annunciation, the meeting between a human and an angel who inhabit very different spiritual realms, and, as a result, they could not (or should not) really be depicted in the same space. You would only know this if you knew at least something about medieval European religion and culture. But even if you had no information about medieval European culture whatsoever, just by noticing the oddities of the spatial relation between these two figures, you would at least be in the position to identify this culturally specific oddity. In order to understand why this is a design problem in medieval Annunciations, you would need to know something about the local (medieval European) culture. But you can notice this design problem without any culture-specific information.

Global aesthetics is based on the mutually strengthening interactions between culturally specific information and very general formal features that every artefact of a certain kind shares. These two seemingly opposite tendencies can and should help each other: the more we find out about some recurring formal feature of the artefacts in a certain culture (for example, whether they deliberately avoid occlusion), the better position we are in to look for some culturally specific information about why they do so.

Even more lost in the museum

I started the book with an experience all of us have when facing works of art or other objects of aesthetic importance—we sometimes just find it difficult to get into the swing of having an aesthetic experience no matter how hard we try. You have had strong and rewarding aesthetic experiences in front of this artwork. But just now it's not happening.

Here is a more specific question that you probably ask yourself in the museum even more often: what should I look for when I am encountering artefacts from different cultures? Take a West African sculpture from Benin (Figure 11). It is highly likely that these sculptures were not meant to be engaged with aesthetically (regardless of how broadly we interpret what counts as aesthetic). What do you do when you enter a room in a museum full of 16th-century Beninese sculptures like this? What kind of experience do you try to have?

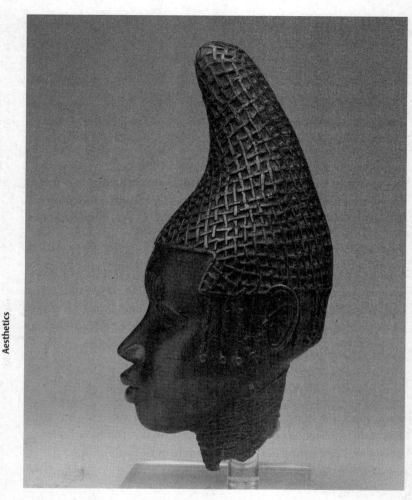

11. *Head of the Queen Mother*, 16th-century (Benin).

My guess is that you are trying to make sense of these objects by relating them to artworks you know. In the case of the West African sculpture, this reference frame is, for many of us, likely to be European modernist sculpture (which, not at all incidentally, was heavily influenced by West African wood carvings). We might be drawn to some sculptures from Benin because they remind us

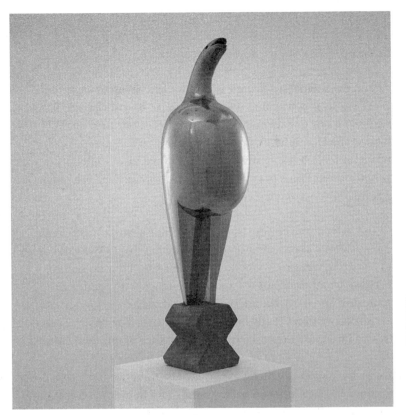

12. Constantin Brâncuşi, *Maiastra* (Guggenheim Museum).

of the modernist sculpture of, say, Constantin Brâncuşi (1876–1957) (Figure 12). And we could take a fair amount of aesthetic pleasure and maybe even aesthetic experience out of this.

I made a sociological claim: I described how we do in fact tend to engage with objects of this kind. But there is a further question: is it wrong if we engage with artefacts in this way? These objects were clearly not meant to be experienced like a Brâncuşi.

A similar question is this: What are we looking for when we encounter artefacts from a different time period? Going to a museum very often implies that you will encounter artefacts from a different time period. Same for listening to music or reading literature. What do we do when we do this?

Again, my sociological claim is that we are trying to experience these works in a way that we can relate to: in ways we are familiar with from our engagement with works from our present. When we look at the Domenico Veneziano painting in Chapter 5, we are trying to look at it in a way that was shaped by our encounter with very different kinds of (say, 20th-century) paintings. The question remains: is it wrong if we do this?

In the light of the culture-specificity of our aesthetic experience, the questions about what's wrong and what's right when it comes to engaging with artworks do not even arise. They do not arise because whether or not it's wrong to engage with Beninese sculpture and early Italian painting as if they were modernist artworks, we don't really have an alternative. The best we can do is to evaluate these artworks from the distance of our own culture.

As we have seen, aesthetic experience is influenced in a top–down manner by one's cultural background. The Beninese sculptor and the people who were the intended audience of the sculptures had very different top–down influences on their aesthetic engagements from the ones I have. This makes it very unlikely that we're engaging in the same way the original producers and users of the artefact did.

But couldn't we at least try to bridge this gap? We could try. And, in some sense, we should. Needless to say, it can be immensely rewarding to learn about other cultures and their artefacts. But there is a systematic reason why full cultural immersion is close to impossible and it is a psychological phenomenon we know very well by now: the mere exposure effect (the repeated exposure to the concept of mere exposure effect throughout this book should really make any reader be positively disposed to it). Because of the mere exposure effect, our value judgements depend on what works we've encountered. Our imprinted aesthetic preferences (dictated by what we have encountered in early formative years) are very, very difficult to shake.

We can spend decades exploring a different culture *in situ*. In fact, this is what many global art historians do. If they research, say, Indonesian art, then they move to Indonesia for many years, even decades, exposing themselves to the cultural milieu, and the stimuli in that milieu that might be very different from the stimuli they are used to. And this can, at least partially, reverse the mere exposure effect. But life is short: even if you get fully immersed in, say, Indonesian culture, you would still be completely lost at an exhibition of Maya art.

Aesthetic humility again

Michael Baxandall (1933–2008), the British art historian and critic, made a distinction between the participants and the observers of a culture. As he says, 'the participant understands and knows [her] culture with an immediacy and spontaneity the observer does not share. [She] can act within the culture's standards and norms without rational self-consciousness.'

My point is that it is very difficult, in fact, close to impossible to fully become participants in a different culture. The default is that we will always remain observers, in spite of all our efforts. Just because we have read a couple of books about Oceanian art, we do not suddenly become participants. And the reason for this is mainly empirical: the top–down influences on perception and the mere exposure effect.

What to do about this? It is still a good idea to read up on distant cultures and forms of art production as it can be immensely rewarding. And global aesthetics should go at least some distance towards understanding how people in other cultures might have seen the world around them. By reading up on distant cultures we can bring them a little bit closer and this can open up thus far unknown aesthetic experiences. But nobody should be deluded into thinking that by doing so we can become participants rather than mere distant observers.

And this gives us even more reason to exercise aesthetic humility. We should always be aware of the cultural perspective that we occupy and treat our aesthetic evaluations with humility: as an evaluation made from a very specific cultural perspective. It is easy to be arrogant about aesthetics—maybe precisely because it matters so much to us personally. But this is all the more reason to be extra careful with our aesthetic evaluations. If there is one take-home message of this book, it is that we all need more aesthetic humility.

References

Chapter 1: Lost in the museum

The Gombrowicz quote is from his *Diaries* (New Haven: Yale University Press, 2012), p. 39.

The Léger story is in his The Machine Aesthetic. *Bulletin de l'effort moderne* (Paris, 1924).

The Newman quote is from John P. O'Neill (ed.), *Barnett Newman: Selected Writings and Interviews* (New York: Alfred A. Knopf, 1990), p. 25.

The 'influential strand in Western aesthetics' goes back to Immanuel Kant's *Critique of Judgement*.

On the importance of the aesthetics of everyday scenes, see Sherri Irvin, The Pervasiveness of the Aesthetic in Ordinary Experience. *British Journal of Aesthetics* 48 (2008): 29–44; Bence Nanay, Aesthetic Experience of Artworks and Everyday Scenes. *The Monist* 101 (2018): 71–82; Yuriko Saito, *Everyday Aesthetics* (Oxford: Oxford University Press, 2007).

Chapter 2: Sex, drugs, and rock 'n' roll

A good exposition of the 'sex, drugs, and rock 'n' roll' problem is in Jerrold Levinson's *The Pleasures of Aesthetics* (Ithaca, NY: Cornell University Press, 1996).

What I call the 'beauty-salon approach' can be found in almost all 'Western' texts on beauty from Plato to Mary Mothersill: see Mary Mothersill, *Beauty Restored* (Oxford: Clarendon Press, 1984).

The Oscar Wilde quote is from his 1879 lecture to art students. In his *Essays and Lectures* (London: Methuen, 1911), p. 111.

A very democratic account of beauty, and one that is broadly congruous with my approach is in Dominic Lopes's *Being for Beauty* (Oxford: Oxford University Press, 2018).

The Léger quote is from: The Machine Aesthetic: The Manufactured Object, the Artisan and the Artist. *Bulletin de l'effort moderne* (Paris, 1924).

For Kant's concept of disinterested pleasure, see Immanuel Kant, *Critique of Judgement*, trans. W. S. Pluhar (Indianapolis: Hackett, 1987, originally 1790).

A good summary of the distinction between restoration pleasure and tonic pleasure is in Michael Kubovy, On the Pleasures of the Mind. In: D. Kahneman, E. Diener, and N. Schwartz (eds), *Well-Being: Foundations of Hedonic Psychology* (New York: Russell Sage Foundation, 1999), pp. 134–49.

The best worked-out account of aesthetic pleasure as sustaining pleasure is Mohan Matthen's theory. See his The Pleasure of Art. *Australasian Philosophical Review* 1 (2017): 6–28. What I call 'relief pleasure', Matthen calls 'r-pleasure' (and Kubovy 'restoration pleasure'); what I call 'sustaining pleasure', Matthen calls 'f-pleasure' (and Kubovy 'tonic pleasure').

Laura Mulvey's article was published in *Screen* 16/3 (1975): 6–18.

The Iris Murdoch quote is from her Existentialist Hero, *The Listener* 23 (March 1950), p. 52.

The Kubler quote is from George Kubler, *The Shape of Time* (New Haven: Yale University Press, 1962), p. 80.

On wonder as an aesthetic emotion, see Jesse Prinz, *Works of Wonder* (New York: Oxford University Press, forthcoming).

On being moved as an aesthetic emotion, see Florian Cova and Julien Deonna, Being Moved. *Philosophical Studies* 169 (2014): 447–66 (although they never make the claim that this is a universal feature of all aesthetic engagement).

On contemplation of formal features as an aesthetic emotion, see Clive Bell, *Art* (London: Chatto and Windus, 1914).

For an argument that all actions are emotional actions, see Bence Nanay, All Actions are Emotional Actions. *Emotion Review* 9 (2017): 350–2.

The quote by Fernando Pessoa is from his *The Book of Disquiet* (London: Serpent's Tail, 1991), p. 27 (29 [87]).

The Sontag quote is in her essay On Style (1965), in her *Against Interpretation* (New York: Farrar Straus Giroux, 1986), p. 27.

A good example of the 'valuing for its own sake' approach is chapter 3 of Robert Stecker's *Aesthetics and Philosophy of Art* (Lanham, Md: Rowman and Littlefield, 2005).

For more on the trophy–process balance, see <https://www.psychologytoday.com/intl/blog/psychology-tomorrow/201812/the-trophy-process-balance>.

The Huxley book is *The Doors of Perception* (London: Chatto and Windus, 1954).

The Proust quote is from his *Sodom and Gomorrah*, chapter II, paragraph 25 (p. 138 in the Moncrieff translation).

Chapter 3: Experience and attention

For some more visual examples of the difference attention can make in your aesthetic and non-aesthetic experiences, see <https://aestheticsforbirds.com/2014/06/16/paying-aesthetic-attention-bence-nanay/>.

The Gorilla experiment: D. J. Simmons and C. F. Chabris, Gorillas in our Midst: Sustained Inattentional Blindness for Dynamic Events. *Perception* 28 (1999): 1059–74. There are some dissenting voices that construe the phenomenon not as inattentional blindness, but as inattentional amnesia (we see the gorilla but then immediately forget that we have seen it). See J. M. Wolfe, Inattentional Amnesia. In: V. Coltheart (ed.), *Fleeting Memories. Cognition of Brief Visual Stimuli* (Cambridge, Mass.: MIT Press, 1999).

A good summary of the psychological research on focused versus distributed attention is in Arien Mack, Is the Visual World a Grand Illusion? *Journal of Consciousness Studies* 9 (2002): 102–10.

For a more detailed account of focused versus distributed attention, see Bence Nanay, *Aesthetics as Philosophy of Perception* (Oxford: Oxford University Press, 2016).

The Danièle Huillet line is from a 2005 interview with Tag Gallagher, *Senses of Cinema*, 2005, Issue 37.

The Maria Abramovic quote is from a 2012 interview with Ross Simonini, *Globe and Mail* 20 February 2012.

The quote by Fernando Pessoa is from his *The Book of Disquiet* (London: Serpent's Tail, 1991), p. 77 (76 [389]).

On the role of experience in Sanskrit aesthetics and Rasa theory in general, see Sheldon Pollock (ed.), *A Rasa Reader* (New York: Columbia University Press, 2016).

A good summary of the transparency of perception is in Laura Gow's The Limitations of Perceptual Transparency. *Philosophical Quarterly* 66 (2016): 723–44.

Chapter 4: Aesthetics and the self

The findings about the importance of aesthetic preferences for the self started with the publication of Nina Strohminger and Shaun Nichols, The Essential Moral Self. *Cognition* 131 (2014): 159–71, and various responses to this paper. See esp. J. Fingerhut, J. Gomez-Lavin, C. Winklmayr, and J. J. Prinz, The Aesthetic Self. In: *Frontiers in Psychology* (forthcoming).

On the findings about the constant changes in our aesthetic preferences, see Cambeon Pugach, Helmut Leder, and Daniel J. Graham, How Stable are Human Aesthetic Preferences across the Lifespan. *Frontiers in Human Neuroscience* 11 (2017): 289. doi: 10.3389/fnhum.2017.00289.

The phenomenon that we think we don't change but we do even has a fancy label, 'The End of History Illusion'. See <https://www.ted.com/talks/bence_nanay_the_end_of_history_illusion>.

The mere exposure effect experiment with the impressionist paintings is reported in James E. Cutting, The Mere Exposure Effect and Aesthetic Preference. In: P. Locher et al. (eds), *New Directions in Aesthetics, Creativity and the Psychology of Art* (New York: Baywood, 2007), pp. 33–46. See also Bence Nanay, Perceptual Learning, the Mere Exposure Effect and Aesthetic Antirealism. *Leonardo* 50 (2017): 58–63.

For a good illustration of how judgement-centred aesthetics is, see Malcolm Budd, Aesthetic Judgements, Aesthetic Principles and Aesthetic Properties. *European Journal of Philosophy* 7/3 (1999): 295–311.

A good exposition of how aesthetics should not bypass talking about the pleasure we take in aesthetic phenomena is Jerrold Levinson's Pleasure and the Value of Works of Art, in his *The Pleasures of Aesthetics* (Ithaca, NY: Cornell University Press, 1996).

The Susan Sontag quote is from her essay On Style (originally published in 1965), reprinted in her *Against Interpretation* (New York: Farrar Straus Giroux, 1986), p. 21.

Hume's essay is Of the Standard of Taste (1757), in *Essays: Moral, Political and Literary*, ed. Eugene Miller (Indianapolis: Liberty, 1985). A very thorough analysis of Hume's argument is in Jerrold

Levinson's Hume's Standard of Taste: The Real Problem. *Journal of Aesthetics and Art Criticism* 60/3 (2002): 227–38.

On the role of experience in Islamic aesthetics, see Valerie Gonzalez, *Beauty and Islam: Aesthetics in Islamic Art and Architecture* (London: I. B. Tauris, 2001). See also J. N. Erzen, Islamic Aesthetics: An Alternative Way to Knowledge. *Journal of Aesthetics and Art Criticism* 65/1 (2007): 69–75.

On the concept of 'tabritu' in Assyro-Babylonian aesthetics, see Irene J. Winter, The Eyes Have It: Votive Statuary, Gilgamesh's Axe, and Cathected Viewing in the Ancient Near East. In: Robert S. Nelson (ed.), *Visuality Before and Beyond the Renaissance: Seeing as Others Saw* (Cambridge: Cambridge University Press, 2000), pp. 22–44.

Chapter 5: Aesthetics and the other

Here is what Pauline Kael said: 'I regard criticism as an art, and if in this country and in this age, it is practised with honesty, it is no more remunerative than the work of an avant-garde film artist.' See her *I Lost It at the Movies: The Essential Kael Collection '54–'65* (London: Marion Boyars, 2002), p. 234.

The Eagleton quote is in his *The Function of Criticism* (London: Verso, 1984), p. 7.

The Malraux line is from André Malraux, *Museum without Walls* (New York: Doubleday, 1967), p. 236.

Chapter 6: Aesthetics and life

The Berenice Abbott quote is from Julia Van Haaften, *Berenice Abbott: A Life in Photography* (New York: W. W. Norton, 2018).

The Robert Musil quip is in his novel *The Man without Qualities*, trans. Eithne Wilkins and Ernst Kaiser (London: Picador, 1979) (1930/2). Volume II, p. 336.

The Camus quote is in his posthumously published *A Happy Death* (New York: Penguin, 2002).

A vivid expression of Oscar Wilde's line on being the spectator of one's own life is in his novel *The Picture of Dorian Grey* (New York: Barnes and Noble, 1995), p. 121.

Arthur Schopenhauer was another influential proponent of the idea of aesthetic contemplation. See esp. his *The World as Will and Representation* (Cambridge: Cambridge University Press, 2011).

The Sontag quote is in her essay On Style (1965), in her *Against Interpretation* (New York: Farrar Straus Giroux, 1986), p. 27.

The André Gide quote is from his *Diary*, 25 July 1934.

The Stendhal quote is in chapter 23 of his novel *Charterhouse of Parma*.

The quote by Giorgio de Chirico is from his 'Meditations of a Painter, 1912'. In Herschel B. Chipp (ed.), *Theories of Modern Art* (Berkeley: University of California Press, 1968), pp. 397–8.

The general idea of art working against our habits is often associated with Russian formalism. See e.g. Victor Shklovsky, 'Art as Technique' (1917). In *Russian Formalist Criticism: Four Essays*, ed. Lee T. Lemon and Marion J. Reis (Lincoln, Nebr.: University of Nebraska Press, 1965). See also Bence Nanay, Defamiliarization and the Unprompted (not Innocent) Eye. *Nonsite* 24 (2018): 1–17.

The Duchamp quote is from Calvin Tomkins, *The Afternoon Interviews* (Brooklyn: Badlands, 2013), p. 55.

The long Proust quote is from *Within a Budding Grove*, trans. C. K. Scott Moncrieff (New York: Vintage, 1970), p. 325.

The Ad Reinhardt quote is from his 'How to Look at Things through a Wine-glass'. *PM*, 7 July 1946.

Chapter 7: Global aesthetics

The De Kooning train-track analogy is from his 'The Renaissance and Order'. *Trans/formation* 1 (1951): 86–7.

For a summary of the literature on top–down influences on perception, see Christoph Teufel and Bence Nanay, How to (and how not to) Think about Top-down Influences on Perception. *Consciousness and Cognition* 47 (2017): 17–25.

For the cross-cultural findings about what we attend to when we are looking at an aquarium, see Takahiko Masuda and Richard E. Nisbett, Attending Holistically versus Analytically: Comparing the Context Sensitivity of Japanese and Americans. *Journal of Personality and Social Psychology* 81 (2001): 922–34.

On mental imagery and the important role it plays in aesthetics, see Bence Nanay, *Seeing Things You Don't See* (Oxford: Oxford University Press, forthcoming).

On the multimodality of our aesthetic experiences in the Rasa tradition, see K. M. Higgins, An Alchemy of Emotion: Rasa and Aesthetic Breakthroughs. *Journal of Aesthetics and Art Criticism*

65/1 (2007): 43–54; see also Bence Nanay, The Multimodal Experience of Art. *British Journal of Aesthetics* 52 (2012): 353–63.

On 'hidden beauty' or Yugen, see T. Izutsu, and T. Izutsu, *The Theory of Beauty in the Classical Aesthetics of Japan* (The Hague: Martinus Nijhoff, 1981). See also Y. Saiko, The Japanese Aesthetics of Imperfection and Insufficiency. *Journal of Aesthetics and Art Criticism* 55/4 (1997): 377–85.

On Avicenna and imagery, see Valerie Gonzales, *Beauty and Islam* (London: I. B. Tauris Publishers, 2001), esp. pp. 16–18.

The Wölfflin quote is from his 1915 *Principles of Art History* (New York: Dover, 1932), p. 11.

More on the history of vision debate in Bence Nanay, The History of Vision. *Journal of Aesthetics and Art Criticism* 73 (2015): 259–71.

On just how much we know about how paintings were looked at in 15th-century Italy, see Michael Baxandall, *Painting and Experience in Fifteenth Century Italy* (Oxford: Oxford University Press, 1972).

On 'ifarahon' and Yoruba aesthetics in general, see Stephen F. Sprague: Yoruba photography. *African Art* 12 (1978): 52–107.

On Xie He's aesthetics of painting, see H. Saussy, *The Problem of a Chinese Aesthetic* (Stanford, Calif.: Stanford University Press, 1993).

The *Vishnudharmottara* is freely available online: Stella Kramrisch, *The Vishnudharmottara Part III: A Treatise on Indian Painting and Image-Making* (Calcutta: Calcutta University Press, 1928).

On pictorial organization in Japanese aesthetics, see Ken-ichi Sasaki, Perspectives East and West. *Contemporary Aesthetics* 11 (2013): spo.7523862.0011.016.

For more on surface and scene pictorial organization, see Bence Nanay, Two-Dimensional versus Three-Dimensional Pictorial Organization. *Journal of Aesthetics and Art Criticism* 73 (2015): 149–57.

The Baxandall quote is from his *Patterns of Intention* (New Haven: Yale University Press, 1985), p. 109.

Further reading

Non-'Western' aesthetics

Heather Ahtone, Designed to Last: Striving towards an Indigenous American Aesthetics. *International Journal of the Arts in Society* 4 (2009): 373–85.

Zainab Bahrani, *The Graven Image: Representation in Babylonia and Assyria* (Philadelphia: University of Pennsylvania Press, 2003).

H. Gene Blocker, Non-Western Aesthetics as a Colonial Invention. *Journal of Aesthetic Education* 35 (2001): 3–13.

Stephen Davies, Balinese Aesthetics. *Journal of Aesthetics and Art Criticism* 65/1 (2007): 21–9.

Susan L. Feagin (ed.), *Global Theories of Art and Aesthetics.* Special issue of *Journal of Aesthetics and Art Criticism* 65/1 (2007).

Dominic Lopes, Shikinen Sengu and the Ontology of Architecture in Japan. *Journal of Aesthetics and Art Criticism* 65 (2007): 77–84.

Philip Rawson, The Methods of Zen Painting. *British Journal of Aesthetics* 7 (1967): 315–38.

Yuriko Saito, The Moral Dimension of Japanese Aesthetics. *Journal of Aesthetics and Art Criticism* 65/1 (2007): 85–97.

Susan P. Walton, Aesthetic and Spiritual Correlations in Javanese Gamelan Music. *Journal of Aesthetics and Art Criticism* 65/1 (2007): 31–41.

Robert Wicks, The Idealization of Contingency in Traditional Japanese Aesthetics. *Journal of Aesthetic Education* 39 (2005): 88–101.

Ajume H. Wingo, African Art and the Aesthetics of Hiding and Revealing. *British Journal of Aesthetics* 38 (1998): 251–64.

Aesthetics and art history/anthropology

Franz Boas, *Primitive Art* (Cambridge, Mass.: Harvard University Press, 1927).

Whitney Davis, *A General Theory of Visual Culture* (Princeton: Princeton University Press, 2011).

Roger Fry, *Vision and Design* (London: Chatto and Windus, 1920).

Clifford Geertz, *The Interpretation of Cultures* (New York: Basic Books, 1973).

Feminist and postcolonial aesthetics

Peg Brand (ed.), *Beauty Matters* (Bloomington, Ind.: Indiana University Press, 2000).

Peg Brand and Mary Devereaux (eds), *Women, Art, and Aesthetics*, Special issue of *Hypatia* 18/4 (2003).

Anne Eaton, Why Feminists Shouldn't Deny Disinterestedness. In: L. Ryan Musgrave (ed.), *Feminist Aesthetics and Philosophy of Art: The Power of Critical Visions and Creative Engagement* (New York: Springer, 2017).

Sherri Irvin, *Body Aesthetics* (Oxford: Oxford University Press, 2016).

Carolyn Korsmeyer, *Gender and Aesthetics* (London: Routledge, 2004).

Paul C. Taylor, *Black is Beautiful: A Philosophy of Black Aesthetics* (New York: Wiley, 2016).

Classic Anglo-American aesthetics

Monroe Beardsley, *Aesthetics*, 2nd edition (Indianapolis: Hackett, 1981).

Edward Bullough, 'Physical Distance' as a Factor in Art and as an Aesthetic Principle. *British Journal of Psychology* 5 (1912): 87–98.

John Dewey, *Art as Experience* (New York: Putnam, 1934).

Frank Sibley, Aesthetic and Nonaesthetic. *The Philosophical Review* 74/2 (1965): 135–59.

Jerome Stolnitz, *Aesthetics and Philosophy of Art Criticism* (New York: Houghton Mifflin, 1960).

Contemporary Anglo-American aesthetics

Malcolm Budd, *Values of Art* (London: Allen Lane, 1995).

Noël Carroll, *Beyond Aesthetics* (Cambridge: Cambridge University Press, 2001).

Diarmuid Costello, Kant and the Problem of Strong Non-perceptual Art. *British Journal of Aesthetics* 53 (2013): 277–98.

Robert Hopkins, *Picture, Image and Experience: A Philosophical Inquiry* (Cambridge: Cambridge University Press, 1998).

Matthew Kieran, *Revealing Art* (London: Routledge, 2005).

John Kulvicki, *On Images: Their Structure and Content* (Oxford: Oxford University Press, 2006).

Derek Matravers, Aesthetic Properties. *Proceedings of the Aristotelian Society* Supplementary Volume 79 (2005): 191–210.

Aaron Meskin, Mark Phelan, Margaret Moore, and Matthew Kieran, Mere Exposure to Bad Art. *British Journal of Aesthetics* 53 (2013): 139–64.

Elisabeth Schellekens, Towards a Reasonable Objectivism for Aesthetic Judgements. *British Journal of Aesthetics* 46/2 (2006): 163–77.

Kendall L. Walton, Categories of Art. *Philosophical Review* 79 (1970): 334–67.

Richard Wollheim, *Painting as an Art* (Princeton: Princeton University Press, 1987).

Nick Zangwill, *The Metaphysics of Beauty* (Ithaca, NY: Cornell University Press, 2001).

"牛津通识读本"已出书目

古典哲学的趣味	福柯	地球
人生的意义	缤纷的语言学	记忆
文学理论入门	达达和超现实主义	法律
大众经济学	佛学概论	中国文学
历史之源	维特根斯坦与哲学	托克维尔
设计，无处不在	科学哲学	休谟
生活中的心理学	印度哲学祛魅	分子
政治的历史与边界	克尔凯郭尔	法国大革命
哲学的思与惑	科学革命	民族主义
资本主义	广告	科幻作品
美国总统制	数学	罗素
海德格尔	叔本华	美国政党与选举
我们时代的伦理学	笛卡尔	美国最高法院
卡夫卡是谁	基督教神学	纪录片
考古学的过去与未来	犹太人与犹太教	大萧条与罗斯福新政
天文学简史	现代日本	领导力
社会学的意识	罗兰·巴特	无神论
康德	马基雅维里	罗马共和国
尼采	全球经济史	美国国会
亚里士多德的世界	进化	民主
西方艺术新论	性存在	英格兰文学
全球化面面观	量子理论	现代主义
简明逻辑学	牛顿新传	网络
法哲学：价值与事实	国际移民	自闭症
政治哲学与幸福根基	哈贝马斯	德里达
选择理论	医学伦理	浪漫主义
后殖民主义与世界格局	黑格尔	批判理论